CW00344208

BLANK CANVAS

BLANK

THE AMAZING STORY OF A WOMAN

CANVAS

WHO AWOKE FROM A COMA TO A LIFE

MARCY

SHE COULDN'T REMEMBER

GREGG

TYNDALE
MOMENTUM®

A Tyndale nonfiction imprint

Visit Tyndale online at tyndale.com.

Visit Tyndale Momentum online at tyndalemomentum.com.

Visit the author's website at marcygreggart.com.

Tyndale, Tyndale's quill logo, *Tyndale Momentum*, and the Tyndale Momentum logo are registered trademarks of Tyndale House Ministries. Tyndale Momentum is a nonfiction imprint of Tyndale House Publishers, Carol Stream, Illinois.

Blank Canvas: The Amazing Story of a Woman Who Awoke from a Coma to a Life She Couldn't Remember

Designed by Dean H. Renninger

Edited by Deborah King

The author gratefully acknowledges Katelyn Beaty for her role in shaping this manuscript.

Published in association with the literary agency of Punchline Agency LLC.

For information about special discounts for bulk purchases, please contact Tyndale House Publishers at csresponse@tyndale.com, or call 1-855-277-9400.

Library of Congress Cataloging-in-Publication Data

A catalog record for this book is available from the Library of Congress.

ISBN 978-1-4964-5037-1

Printed in the United States of America

28	27	26	25	24	23	22
7	6	5	4	3	2	1

For Dev, the love of my life—
who's been by my side before, during, and after.

CONTENTS

FOREWORD

I haven't met Marcy yet, but after reading the pages of this book, I can imagine what our first coffee date together will be like. I can see her sitting across from me, telling me this story (the one you're holding in your hands right now), and pointing out the faithfulness of God woven throughout—like intricate golden threads that hold it all together. I can imagine her selflessness and her bravery. I can imagine the ways she'd push me to keep going on a day when I feel like giving up.

That's what it will feel like as you sit down to read this compelling, can't-put-down story about the sacredness of second chances: as if you're having a coffee date with a new-yet-trusted friend.

We talk about those second chances all the time, but it's rare that a story so beautifully illustrates what it looks like to bank on them—day after day, hour by hour, moment to moment. Marcy lives in the second chance, and she inspires her readers to step in fully to the life that is waiting for them.

In our culture today, it is far too easy to check out of our own lives and lose ourselves in the lives of people we don't know. It has never been more tempting to numb ourselves by becoming a spectator of other people's stories, or to allow our own pain to define us for the long haul. But that's not the answer, Marcy reminds us. If you're feeling tired and just wanting to check out, these pages will give you a better route to take.

This is the kind of book that will remind you how the Lord's mercy is new each morning. It's a book that will call you to awake from slumber and look around at your one life to ask some hard questions: *How can I be present within this day? Regardless of my past, how can I show up to build into my future?*

Marcy doesn't claim to have all the answers, and that's honestly one of the most refreshing elements of her storytelling. Throughout the pages of this book, she clings to God, prays honest prayers, and finds the strength each day to keep showing up. She's always pointing to something bigger than herself, and that's the takeaway you'll find yourself wanting to pocket again and again. She takes the blank canvas given to her—as we all must—and she simply decides to paint a life upon it that is a vibrant reflection of his glory.

I pray the words on these pages will serve as a fresh cloak of inspiration draped over your tired spirit. I pray they will show you that God is present in the hard, and he's sovereign in the storms. More than anything, I pray this story will shake you awake to the life you have right in front of you. That instead of choosing to check out, you will start to ask yourself: what would it look like to relentlessly check *in* to my life? To show up and claim it, despite not knowing what the future holds?

You have a blank canvas sitting right in front of you. It might be time to do something with it.

Hannah Brencher
author of Fighting Forward *and* Come Matter Here

PROLOGUE

I gazed around the gallery in sheer wonderment. The gray skies and gentle patter of raindrops against the windows stood in stark contrast to the warm, welcoming lights of the hall, its pristine white walls blanketed in large canvases generously layered with oil paint in various hues, some vibrantly contrasted, others subtle and ethereal—but all purposefully mixed and chosen to accomplish the final composition. The click of my heels against the dark concrete floor echoed throughout the empty space as I slowly took in each of the brightly colored works of art—*my art*.

In less than an hour, the gallery would be filled with the familiar faces of family and friends, all gathering to celebrate my first solo show: *Expressions of Joy*.

What a perfect name, I mused, picking up one of the beautifully printed cards the gallery had created for tonight's reception—thirty-five exact miniatures of the bright, expansive canvases that graced the walls—more than a year of passion, dedication, and inspiration captured in pigment and oil.

I took a deep breath and smiled. It was one of the happiest moments I'd experienced, building on the many joy-filled hours I'd spent in the studio, bringing this show to life—the crisp, slightly citrusy scent of linseed oil permeating the air, light pouring in through the windows, the soft, cushiony feel of the Berber fibers beneath my bare feet, my hands and apron flecked with various hues of yellow, blue, orange, red, and green. I never felt more alive than I did when I was painting. It was almost like a form of worship—a beautiful, pure, spontaneous *expression of joy*.

I made my way to the center of the gallery, where my favorite piece was prominently displayed—a massive 72 x 48 in. abstract called *Lost and Found*. I walked up to the canvas, reached out my hand, and gently traced one of the delicate ridges left behind by the palette knife, my lips curving into a smile at the hidden message that lay beneath the thick layers of golden ochre and titanium white, contrasted by faint hues of cerulean blue. Most striking of all was the not-so-subtle pop of deep crimson carefully placed to grab your eye. It was the heartbeat of the piece, bringing life to all the other colors.

My eyes traveled across the canvas to the description of my work, just to the right of the painting:

> Marcy Gregg's paintings are multifaceted explorations of the intrinsic beauty of form and color and the inherent properties of her chosen medium, fine oil paints. Gregg's creative compositions, whether representational or abstract, reflect her love of color and texture. Frequently she builds layer upon layer of paint to create a thick application that is then finished by the use of a palette knife.

I closed my eyes in the church-like silence, my heart filled with gratitude. *God . . . you did this. Thank you.* Thunder rolled in the distance. *Now, if you could do something about this weather . . .*

"Marcy!"

I quickly spun around to see Anne Neilson, the owner of the gallery, approaching. Anne and I had met in a Bible study, and our mutual passion for art resulted in an almost instant friendship. Anne had received national acclaim for her oil paintings of angels, and she donated a portion of the proceeds from each of her sales to charitable causes, which I loved. Her book had recently been featured on the *Today* show, after Kathie Lee Gifford used one of Anne's angel paintings on her personal Christmas card. She had seen some of my work in a local fundraiser, and when I told her about my somewhat unorthodox underpainting and layering technique, she invited me to join her gallery in the trendy South End neighborhood in downtown Charlotte. And her timing could not have been more perfect because I had recently left my first Charlotte gallery and was now unrepresented and available.

When Anne offered to host a solo show on my behalf, I was both honored and slightly petrified. It was one thing to have strangers view my work online or at a charity event, but it was another thing entirely to have friends and family admiring it up close, which might have explained the goose bumps that had suddenly appeared on my bare arms.

"So . . ." Anne smiled brightly. "Are you ready?"

I took a deep breath. "I think so." I glanced around the room one more time. "Everything looks so beautiful. Thank you, Anne. And these . . ." I held up one of the cards she had printed. "These are amazing!"

"Oh, you're so welcome, Marcy," she said, rubbing the goose bumps from my arms. "Come on." She grabbed my hand and led me toward the reception area. "People will be arriving soon."

Sure enough, as soon as we got there, Christine, our longtime nanny and housekeeper, burst through the door, umbrella first.

"Tinie! I can't believe you came!" I could already feel the tears starting to form. This was going to be a long but beautiful evening.

"Are you kidding? I wouldn't miss this for the world!" She beamed, pulling me into a huge hug. Then she stepped back and scanned the room. "Where are Dev and the kids?"

"Oh, they'll be here," I assured her. "Dev is bringing Conner and Callie, and Casen's flying in from Dallas. His plane should be landing any minute," I said, glancing up at the clock. "Can I give you a personal tour?"

"You may!" She smiled back.

"You two go ahead," Anne said. "I'll let you know when the others arrive."

Truth be told, I was grateful Tinie had arrived early. Having her there helped calm my nerves. She just had that effect. She had been a good friend and trusted confidante since the boys were little, before we even had Callie. I couldn't imagine what my life would have looked like without her.

I was just showing Tinie one of my favorite paintings, a large 60 x 60 in. abstract with splashes of deep yellow ochre peeking out from layers of grays and delicate ivories, with faint lines forming a subtle cross, titled *Called by Love*, when Anne poked her head around the corner.

"Marcy, Dev just pulled up."

"Don't worry about me," Tinie said, waving me off. "Go!"

I arrived just in time to find Dev, holding the gallery door open with one arm, and his blazer over his head with the other, leaving just enough space for our son Conner, our daughter, Callie, and her boyfriend, Joseph, to rush in from the rain.

"Callie, you should have a coat on!" I brushed a stray wisp of blonde hair from her eyes.

"I'm fine, Mom," she assured me. "It's not cold out—just wet."

She did look beautiful in flowing black slacks and a bright orange sleeveless top that showed off her tanned shoulders. And Conner looked so handsome in his dress khakis and blue blazer. Not surprisingly, neither he nor Dev had bothered with a tie.

Like father, like son.

Conner leaned down and kissed me on the cheek. "Hey, Mom, congratulations. Everything looks great." He smiled brightly, revealing the trademark dimple I'd always loved.

"Thank you, sweetie."

As the kids made their way into the gallery, I turned to Dev. "I hope Casen and Megan get here on time with this weather."

"I'm sure they'll be fine," he assured me. "How about you? How are you holding up?"

"Nervous. Excited," I said, brushing the wrinkles out of his white button-down shirt.

He smiled at me, his deep-set blue eyes crinkling in the corners. "Don't worry. Everything's going to be okay. I love you."

My breath caught in my chest. He had no idea how much I needed to hear that.

"Can I get you anything?" he asked.

"A Diet Coke?" I suggested.

"You've got it."

By the time he came back, the lightly falling rain had turned into a full-on downpour, just as more cars were lining up outside the entrance. Seeing the concern on my face, Dev handed me my drink and said, "I'll be back." Then, in a brand-new pair of dress shoes, he dashed around puddle after puddle to our car to get a golf umbrella, and one by one, escorted our guests up to the front door, delivering them safe and sound.

"You've got yourself quite a guy there," Anne remarked.

"You have no idea." I smiled absently, watching Dev look after our friends.

Before long, the gallery was alive with chatter. I couldn't believe how many people showed up, and on such a terrible night—neighbors, people from church—everywhere I looked, I was met with the smiling faces of people who, over the years, Dev and I had come to think of as family. I was completely overwhelmed. Then, from the back of the room, I heard yet another familiar voice.

"Mom!"

I turned toward the door to find our oldest son, Casen, standing next to his girlfriend, Megan. He had the same sandy blond hair mussed off to the side and square-set jaw as his dad. In fact so much of Casen reminded me of Dev.

"Look who we ran into outside." He stepped aside to reveal my mom, my younger sister Ann, and her son, David.

We all exchanged hugs and kisses, then Casen and Megan disappeared into the crowd with David to find Conner and Callie.

"Mom, you look so beautiful." I stood back to admire the bright yellow, black, and white top she was wearing, impeccably set off by a double-strand of pearls and small gold hoop earrings. And as usual, her makeup was perfect. My eyes filled with tears, and I pulled her into another embrace.

"Oh, darling, your daddy would be so proud of you," she whispered.

"I know . . ." I choked back a sob. "I wish he could have seen this."

"I know, darling," she said, rubbing my back. "He would have loved it."

"And I'm sure he'd be thrilled that for once you weren't making a mess of his driveway," Ann joked—a well-timed allusion to my childhood penchant for covering Dad's normally pristine driveway with massive chalk art designs.

I pulled out of Mom's embrace and turned to Ann, who looked positively gorgeous, like a younger version of Mom, with shoulder-length mahogany-colored hair and the most beautiful hazel eyes God ever gifted anyone.

"Marcy, this is beautiful," she beamed, taking in the room.

I could feel the tears forming again. "Well . . . don't just stand there," I urged, anxious to take the focus off of me. "Go take a look around." I shooed them off and took a deep breath, hoping against all hope my waterproof mascara would live up to its name.

As if on cue, as soon as Dev ushered in the last of the guests, the skies cleared, and I wandered throughout the gallery talking, laughing, visiting with friends, and answering questions about my art and the hidden messages behind each picture.

"This is so amazing, Mom!" Callie called out from in front of a light orange and cobalt blue composition that complemented her outfit perfectly.

"Thank you, sweetheart."

"Hey, did you all see Mom's bio?" Conner asked, pointing up at the floor-to-ceiling graphic Anne had placed alongside *Lost and Found*. "It's so cool to see it written out!"

I quickly skimmed the text, though I knew it all by heart. It was so strange to see my entire life encapsulated like that. Even though I had long since come to grips with what had happened to me—to us—twenty-five years ago, I knew it was difficult for others to wrap their heads around it. How could they? Things like that just don't happen. Until they do.

"Good evening," Anne spoke over the crowd, and the lively chatter hushed. "My name is Anne Neilson, and I'd like to welcome you all here tonight to celebrate the first solo show of one of Charlotte's most exciting new artists and my good friend, Marcy Gregg."

I lowered my head as a polite round of applause filled the room. Dev squeezed my hand and winked at me.

"I know many of you here tonight know Marcy and are aware of her story—"she gestured toward the write-up behind her—"but for those of you who aren't . . . well . . ." She smiled knowingly. "You're in for a real treat. Marcy, would you like to come up, please, and say a few words?"

I nodded, gave Dev's hand a final squeeze, and took my place in front of *Lost and Found*, my heart beating like a rabbit. Once my eyes swept over the room, however, and I saw all the faces of my family, neighbors, and friends smiling back at me, my heart settled, and I found myself overcome with gratefulness.

"Well, first, I'd like to thank you all so much for coming out on such a terrible night. Seeing all of you gathered here together just means the world to me, and I can assure you, I'll never forget it." A few knowing chuckles echoed throughout the room.

"For those of you who don't know me, my name is Marcy Gregg. I'm sure many of you have already met my husband, Dev, who graciously brought many of you in out of the rain."

Dev smiled sheepishly and waved his hand as a polite smattering of applause and laughter ensued.

"I was born in a small town in East Texas. I went to Southern Methodist University in Dallas, where I majored in art. My freshman year, I met the man who would eventually become my husband." I winked at Dev. "After we got married, I was away from art for years. I worked and then focused on raising my family. We had two little boys." I smiled at Casen and Conner. "Then we moved to Charlotte. And, when I was thirty, I gave birth to a little girl." I met Callie's gaze and she smiled brightly at me.

I took a deep breath. "And that's where my story gets a little crazy . . ."

PART 1

FACES

I

ONCE

KNEW

CHAPTER 1

OUT OF FOCUS

MARCH 1990

I opened my eyes, and pain radiated throughout my neck and skull.

I looked down and strained to focus my eyes. I was lying in a long bed with shiny metal rails. Covered in translucent tubes, my arms lay limp and frail on a heap of crumpled white sheets. My hands looked shriveled and curled into fists. Every limb felt as though it was glued in place.

I tried to raise my head a few inches but was exhausted by the effort.

I looked a couple of inches to the left, then right. A white gauzy curtain reached to the ceiling, and a series of piercing monotonous beeps punctuated the ringing in my ears. I could hear voices in the distance, but it all seemed shrouded in fog.

I tried to blink the fog away, but nothing came into focus.

Where am I?

I closed my eyes, exhausted from my few brief moments of consciousness, and everything went dark.

———

I opened my eyes again, and a light stench of antiseptic combined with a whiff of sweat hit my nostrils, causing my stomach to churn.

The beeping persisted. I looked to the right. A few feet from the bed, a black screen flashed lines and numbers. Beneath it, rows of knobs turned at different angles were attuned to some indiscernible frequency.

I tried to gulp down a breath, but it caught in my chest. It felt as though I had swallowed a beehive.

Water. I need water.

I tried to speak, but the words got stuck somewhere between my brain and my lips.

Can somebody help me, please?

I looked down and noticed that there were straps around my wrists—circles of Velcro fabric fastened to the sides of the bed like handcuffs. I tried to lift my arms, but the straps held them flat.

I was trapped. My heart quickened.

I need to get up. Now.

The pain in my head radiated throughout every limb like red-hot flares every time I tried to move even a few inches.

I was frightened.

I was alone.

Then . . . a familiar face.

It's a clock!

It had a white face with black hands and numbers. Plain yet reassuring. Familiar. Only . . .

What does it say? Why can't I . . . ?

I stared at its hands for what felt like hours, but no matter how hard I tried I couldn't get the numbers to focus. And inside that windowless room, there was no way to tell what time it was. It could have been a bright sunny afternoon or the dead of night. Once again, exhausted from the effort, I closed my eyes.

⌒

Something jostled me awake. I could hear muffled voices coming from behind the door in the corner of the room, followed by the sound of footsteps and the squeak of rubber on linoleum.

The door opened and two young women came in, murmuring to each other, their voices soft and low. They were wearing blue cotton V-necks and matching pants, their hair pulled back in ponytails. The first woman was carrying a clipboard. The other examined the clear tube coming from the crook of my elbow. Every time she touched it, a wave of pain shot through my arm.

Water. Please, I need water.

"Patient's name is Marcy Gregg. Age thirty," the second woman said. "She was recently extubated and woke up this morning." She turned to me and smiled faintly.

"We're so glad to see you doing better, Marcy."

Marcy? The name echoed in my mind. It was the strangest sounding name I had ever heard. A discordant note in my ears.

"Are you experiencing any pain?"

I tried to speak, but only a guttural noise came out.

"I'm sure you're glad to have that tube out of your throat."

I searched the woman's eyes for an explanation—some hint of what was going on.

"It probably hurts. You've been on a ventilator for several days." She rolled up my right sleeve. "We need to check your blood pressure, heart rate, and oxygen level, okay, Marcy?"

She wrapped a heavy band around my arm. With every squeeze,

the band became tighter until it almost became unbearable. I turned my head and tried to focus on the clock's hands. They moved like molasses.

". . . and we're done. Blood pressure is 129 over 74. Slightly elevated heart rate—106 BPMs." The other woman jotted down more notes. "We're going to up your fluids, Marcy. That will help bring your heart rate down. Just keep taking deep breaths. That's your only job right now. You're doing so much better than a few hours ago."

I tried to do what she said, but every breath hurt.

"Dr. Brawley will come in to check on you too."

The woman with the clipboard looked up from her notes. "Your husband was here when you woke up, Marcy," she said. "You might not remember. He'll be back soon. He just needed to shower and rest a little."

Husband? Panic bubbled to the surface. *But . . . I'm not married.*

"You've been through a lot," she said reassuringly, "but the worst is over. You're going to be okay."

I closed my eyes tight, fighting back tears. I was trapped, alone, in pain. Nothing in my body seemed to be working right—and nothing anyone said made sense.

When my eyes fluttered open again, every inch, from head to toe, felt tender, like I had been churned up in a food processor. I had no idea how long it had been since I first woke.

I need to get out of this bed.

I peered up and saw the clock staring back at me. I still couldn't read it—the numbers and hands just would not come into focus. Just then, the door clicked open and the woman with the clipboard poked her head in.

"The doctor is here to see you, Marcy."

An older man wearing bifocals sauntered into the room. A blue collar and red tie peeked out from beneath a sharp white coat that hung to his knees. There was small writing in stitching above the breast pocket.

He walked to the end of the bed. He looked confident, like he was in charge of the place. "Hello, Marcy. It's good to see you finally awake."

There's that name again.

"I'm one of the doctors who has been working with you. You wouldn't remember me, but I've been monitoring your progress for several days." He reached down into the pocket of his white coat and pulled out a small black flashlight. "Tilt your head up a bit if you can and look straight ahead."

I strained to hold my neck up.

He moved the flashlight slowly back and forth between my eyes.

"Good. Just keep looking straight."

Is there something wrong with my eyes? I held my gaze on the clock, the clock that was a blur of grayish numbers.

He clicked the flashlight off, put it back in his coat pocket, and I let my head fall back on the pillow.

"Good. Your pupils are dilating and constricting—that's a good sign."

But I can't move or talk.

"And can you move your fingers and toes for me?" the doctor asked.

I looked down at my hands, which were still clenched in fists. With effort, I moved my pointer fingers a few centimeters, then looked down toward my feet. I could see small movements under the sheets.

"Good. Now, you might be a bit confused about how you got here."

I looked at him pleadingly.

"Several days ago, you gave birth to a baby girl."

What?! That couldn't be right. There was no way I could have given birth. I wasn't even married.

"It was a normal delivery. The baby is as healthy as can be. She's being taken care of in the nursery downstairs, but during the delivery, some bacteria got into your bloodstream and infected the membranes in your brain. We believe it was pneumococcal bacterial meningitis . . . a severe, potentially fatal brain infection. We did everything we could to intervene, but the infection became so severe that you slipped into a coma."

Coma. The word sent a chill down my spine.

"We had to drill a hole in your skull to relieve the pressure in your brain."

A hole in my skull? Is that why it hurts so bad?

"I know it sounds alarming," he said calmly, "but it's a normal procedure to relieve swelling on the brain. Nothing out of the ordinary for someone in your situation."

I tried to process what the doctor was saying, but the pain in my head made thinking difficult.

"We've been working day and night to stabilize you. Right now you're probably a little disoriented."

I nodded, and pain shot down my neck.

"But we're going to do all we can to make sure you continue to improve, okay?"

I nodded again, more gently this time.

"Good. I'm just going to ask you a few simple questions. Do you know your name?"

I blinked. Everyone kept calling me Marcy. I rolled the word around in my mind to see if it rang a bell, but nothing about it was familiar. I stared back at the doctor blankly.

He reached up above my head, pulled down a white sheet of paper, and flipped it around so that I could see the big red script on it. I couldn't make out the words. It looked like scribbles.

"Here it is," he said. "See? It says PATIENT GOES BY THE NAME MARCY."

Nothing.

"Okay. Can you tell me your date of birth?"

I couldn't even hazard a guess. For some reason 1960 felt right, though why, I couldn't say.

I shook my head.

"That's okay," he smiled reassuringly. "Let me ask another way. Do you know how old you are?"

The last thing I remembered was starting my freshman year of college at Southern Methodist University in Dallas. That meant I must have been . . .

I opened my mouth and croaked out a single word. "Seventeen." The word burned my throat.

The doctor furrowed his brows. "No, Marcy. You're thirty."

Thirty? That couldn't be right. How could I be thirty?

"That's enough for now," he said. "Don't worry, Marcy. As the swelling in your brain goes down, things will begin to make more sense. For now, just get some rest. The worst is behind you."

As the doctor left the room, I slumped back even farther into my pillow. *What in the world is happening to me?*

CHAPTER 2

COMFORT AND CONFUSION

I opened my eyes at the sound of the door clicking open again. The woman with the clipboard poked her head in, smiled at me, then turned to someone outside the door and said, "It's okay, she's awake."

A man with dark hair and sparkling eyes came out from behind her and walked slowly toward my bed. He had silver at his temples, wrinkles around his eyes, and a smile that lit up the small, dim room like a Christmas tree.

I recognized that smile.

Dad.

Finally, someone I knew.

He bent over to look at me, and his eyes held me in their embrace. He took my right hand in his, being careful not to disturb the tubes. As he stood there, gently caressing my palm and wrist, my heart settled in. I took another breath and felt the air go deep into my lungs.

"I love you," he said. "Everything is going to be okay."

The truth of his words fell like a stone in the well of my fear. He had said this so many times before.

A memory bubbled up from the muck of confusion. I was nine years old and had a bone tumor. Dad was holding my hand, standing between me and Mom as we walked down the hospital corridor. She was going to donate bone from her hip to replace the tumorous bone in my arm. I was nervous about the surgery. Dad noticed the fear in my eyes and said, "Everything is going to be okay."

As a dentist, Dad knew medicine. He had walked hospital corridors before. He could fix anything. When I scraped my knee on the playground, I ran to him for a kiss and a Band-Aid. When I had a fever, he made it go away. And every time I had been in a medical crisis, he had been right: everything always turned out okay.

I smiled up at him with my eyes. I so wanted to talk to him, to ask him what had happened to me, but my throat felt as though it was bleeding with every swallow.

He clung to my hand for some time, and I held on.

As I pleaded with my eyes for him to get me out of this mess, the woman with the clipboard reappeared in the doorway.

"It's time to go, Dr. Perkins," she said.

He squeezed my hand once more before turning to leave.

No, Dad. Don't go. I need you.

Crestfallen, I watched him follow her back through the doorway. As he left, another man wearing khakis and a striped, button-down polo walked into the room.

"Someone else is here to see you, Marcy," the woman said.

The man had a sweet smile across his face, and as he came toward me, he took slow steps, as if I were a frightened deer that would have bolted at any sudden movement. His blue eyes were moist and creased in the corners, with dark crescent-shaped bags underneath. His blond hair was mussed to the side.

As he leaned in closer, I could see his eyes were bloodshot, like it had been days since he last slept. He gently reached down to hold my face, tilting my chin up a bit, and I realized he was going to kiss me.

Wait! Who is this man?

I was too weak to turn my head or protest. His lips landed on my forehead, and just as quickly, the man moved away.

He pulled a folding chair up next to my bed, sat down, and breathed deeply as if he had just finished carrying a boulder up a mountain. When he reached for my hand, I noticed a gold wedding band.

His eyes started to mist. "I'm so glad you're back. We thought we'd lost you." The corners of his eyes crinkled with worry. "Are you thirsty?" he asked.

I moved my head up and down a bit, my neck stiff as a pipe.

He turned and asked the nurse standing near the doorway for water. As we waited, he reached for my hand again, gently holding it there for a few moments.

I stared at him, brows creased, trying to find something familiar in the shape of his features. I was fairly certain he wasn't a doctor. At least he wasn't dressed like the doctor who had been in my room before. Besides, doctors don't usually kiss their patients. But the fogginess that filled my mind only deepened the harder I tried to place him.

He took a deep breath. "Marcy," he asked hesitantly, "do you know who I am?"

My mind raced, but I found nothing to latch on to. And I was so tired . . .

"Honey, it's me, Dev," he said gently.

Dev . . . Dev. Something about it rang like an echo. Someone I used to know? A friend from high school? An old neighbor?

"Do you know why you're here?" he asked.

I remembered what the doctor had told me—I delivered a baby . . . then I got sick . . . I fell into a coma . . . they had to drill a hole—but strung together, none of the words made sense.

"Marcy, I'm your husband. You gave birth to our baby girl, Callie, several days ago."

I swallowed hard. *Our baby girl.* My hands started to feel clammy. Sweat beaded on my brow. My body was so light and weak, I felt like the bed might swallow it up.

"The night before you were supposed to come home, the nurses found you delirious with fever. They called Dr. DeHoff, your OB, and then he called Charles Ferree. Do you remember him?"

Another name I didn't recognize. I shook my head.

"Dr. Charles Ferree—he is our friend. He practices internal medicine. He ordered a spinal tap to identify the infection, then he called me. I drove as fast as I could, but by the time I got here you were already in the coma."

Dev's shoulders suddenly slumped, and his head hung low, as if he had the weight of the world on his back. "They called in so many doctors," he continued. "An infectious disease specialist, a neurologist, a neurosurgeon . . . There were so many people crammed into this room, I could barely keep track of everyone. Just last night, we all thought . . ." He shuddered a bit and shook his head. "I'm just so grateful they moved so quickly."

The nurse walked over to the bed. "Here's some water for her."

Dev took the plastic cup and brought the straw to my lips. It quenched the fire in my throat. I took several sips until the cup was empty then let my head sink back into the pillow.

He squeezed my hand, as if holding it would keep me from slipping away again. He looked as exhausted as I felt. I still couldn't remember him, but he obviously cared for me deeply.

But that name . . . *Dev* . . . there was something familiar about it.

"We've all been so worried about you," he said, brushing a stray hair from my forehead.

The nurse peeked her head back in the doorway.

"Mr. Gregg, we'll let you see Marcy again soon, but now she needs to rest."

He nodded at the nurse, looked at me, and sighed. Then he leaned over and kissed me on the cheek. It felt just as strange as the first kiss.

"I'll be back soon. I promise. I love you."

I tried to smile, but my head was spinning as I watched him leave—this man whom I had never seen before, who said that he loved me, that we were married, and that we had a baby together.

I squeezed my eyes tight and choked back a sob.

Sometime later, two older gentlemen wearing white doctors' jackets came in, trailed by one of the nurses. The three of them stood in a semicircle at the foot of my bed, talking quietly among themselves. They were no more than six feet away, but it felt as though they were on the other side of a glass wall.

One of the doctors rested his arms on the metal edge of the bed.

"We're glad to see you off the ventilator," he said.

I strained to lift my head a bit, pain radiating through my skull, down my neck, and into my spine. I was determined to ask them some questions, even though I knew it would take every bit of energy I had just to speak. I opened my mouth, and my throat burned as I waited for the words to come.

"Why . . . am I here?" My voice sounded raspy, like a rusty engine struggling to start.

They looked at one another then back at me, their expressions blank. Then the one leaning on my bed spoke.

"Several days ago, you gave birth to a baby, here, at this hospital."

"I *did not* have a baby." My voice quavered.

"Yes, Marcy. You did," he pressed gently. "You gave birth to a baby girl several days ago."

There was so much I wanted to say, but I had neither the physical nor the emotional stamina to get it all out. It was as though I was trapped in a bad dream and everyone was in on the plot except me. How could I have had a baby when I'd never even been married? Or pregnant? I'd never even had sex!

Then I remembered . . . *Dad.*

Oh my gosh . . . does Dad think I had a baby? I was mortified at the thought.

"I did *not* have a baby," I repeated. "I'm only seventeen. And I'm a virgin."

One of the doctors raised his eyebrows and cleared his throat.

"Marcy, you're not seventeen. You're thirty years old."

My head was swimming. That's what the other doctor had said. But how could that be? If I was thirty years old, what happened to all those extra years? Why couldn't I remember nearly half of my life? Tears burned my eyes.

"Marcy," he continued, "we're not entirely sure why you think you're seventeen—why your brain came out of the coma 'reset' at that particular age. We believe the memory loss is due to the swelling in your brain. As it goes down, your memory will start to return. Honestly," he shook his head, "it's a miracle you're still with us. We told your husband . . ."

"I don't have a husband," I croaked, desperate.

"Yes, you do, Marcy," he said gently. "He's been here ever since you slipped into the coma. He refuses to leave. You've seen him. Dev Gregg?" He looked at me expectantly.

Dev. The man who had been here before, kissed my cheek, held my hand. My mind raced.

"Marcy," the doctor continued, "do you know where you are?"

"Baylor Hospital," I said confidently, "in Dallas." That much I did know. I'd passed it dozens of times. It was only a few miles away from campus.

He shook his head. "No, Marcy. You're at Presbyterian Hospital in Charlotte, North Carolina."

That was impossible. I'd never even been to Charlotte. I closed my eyes. Nothing they were telling me made any sense—the baby, the coma, Charlotte, not even my own name. Everybody seemed so sure of themselves, so confident in the facts they were presenting. So why couldn't I remember any of it? Hot tears began cascading down my cheeks.

"You've been through a lot," the doctor said, resting his hand on my shoulder. "Try not to worry yourself. It will all come back to you. For now just get some rest. We'll be back to see how you're doing a little later, okay?"

I nodded and swallowed hard, forcing dozens of unasked questions deep into my core. The nurse pulled the door closed as they left, leaving it open just a sliver. And just like that, I was alone. My body started to shake, and before I knew it, I was sobbing. It was all just too much—the pain, the confusion—all of it.

I looked up at the clock—the only face I recognized. *No*, I quickly caught myself. It wasn't the only one. *Dad.* I had recognized Dad. I pictured his face, careworn and concerned, and my breathing slowed a little. Before he left, he had told me that everything was going to be okay. He had promised. He had made the same promise when I scraped my knee, when I had a fever, and when I had the bone tumor, and every time, he had been right.

Oh please, God, I prayed through tears, *let him be right again.*

CHAPTER 3

A MOTHER OF THREE

"Babe?"

I opened my eyes again to see the man with the warm smile and the sandy blond hair from before.

Dev.

I had to admit, he was a better sight to wake up to than the clock on the wall. I also had to admit, he was very attractive. In fact, if he wasn't so much older than me . . .

"Marcy," he said, taking my hand. "I know things are a little fuzzy right now, but it's okay. We're going to get through this. Together."

It still hurt to talk, and for once, I was grateful, because I honestly didn't know what to say. Even though I couldn't remember him, I had no reason to believe he was lying. Everyone kept telling me my memory was hazy because of the coma. Maybe they were right. Maybe I really *was* thirty. Maybe I *did* know this man.

"You remember Casen and Conner," he asked hopefully, "our little boys?"

Casen and Conner? *I have* three *kids with this man?*

I gave Dev a faint smile, hoping that would be enough to melt away the worry that flashed across his face at my lack of recognition, but my heart was racing so quickly, I worried he would be able to see it pounding right through the sheets.

"Don't worry, sweetie," he said reassuringly. "The doctors said your memory will get better as the swelling goes down."

Would it? I wondered. Nothing had come back yet—except Dad. I could see forgetting little things, like getting sick or going to the hospital, but getting married? Having children? *What kind of mother doesn't remember her own kids? And where on earth did we get those names?*

"In fact," he said, fumbling for something in his breast pocket, "one of the nurses had an idea."

He pulled out a few glossy pieces of paper and a roll of tape. "I brought you some photos of the kids." He looked helplessly at the nurse. "Where would be a good place to put these?"

"Here, let me help you," she said, taking the tape from Dev. "We can tape them up here. That way she can see them, but they won't be in the way."

As Dev and the nurse attached four glossy photos to the rail on the left side of the bed, I squinted to make out the images, but it was no use. Everything looked blurry, as though someone had smeared Vaseline over my eyes.

"There we go," said Dev, admiring his work. "Your mom and dad will be bringing them here to see you soon. They've taken such great care of them these past few days."

I closed my eyes and tried to remember, but all I saw was darkness. When I looked back up, Dev's eyes were filled with tears.

That poor man. I wanted so badly to remember him.

To remember the little boys in the pictures.

To remember anything.

⌐

"Darling . . . ? Darling . . . ?"

The sweet voice was soothing, like a warm blanket enveloping me on a cold winter evening.

"Marcy, darling."

My eyes fluttered open. In a chair pulled up to the side of my bed sat a woman with perfectly applied lipstick and short, wavy hair the color of mahogany. Dressed in a beautiful floral top and small gold hoop earrings, she looked completely out of place against the backdrop of the dim hospital room. Tears pooled in her eyes.

"Mom . . ." I croaked.

"Yes, sweetheart. I'm here." Her voice broke as she rested her hand on my arm.

Mom's touch was like a balm, healing with every caress. With her by my side, my heartbeat fell into a steady patter. With Dad, I felt strength. With Mom, I felt soothed. From Dad, I had always drawn confidence, from Mom, solace. A good combination right about now. I took a deep breath.

Her eyes glistened as she peered into mine. "I love you."

"I love you too, Mom." My voice was little more than a whisper.

As I examined her face, I could see that her brow was knitted. Then it clicked. Everything the doctors had said—the infection, the coma, the hole in my skull—Mom must have been terrified. Dad, too. To see their daughter draped in tubes from head to toe, unconscious for days.

"Mom . . ." I looked pleadingly into her eyes. "Please don't leave me."

"I won't," she said. "I'll always be here for you, Marcy."

She reached up and gently massaged my scalp with her fingers, and for the first time in what felt like days, the pain in my forehead and neck eased up a bit.

"I'm so glad you're here . . ." My voice broke.

Her mouth curved into a smile. "You have such a beautiful little baby girl waiting to meet you downstairs."

My heart sank. I had almost forgotten.

"Callie." Mom beamed as she brushed a piece of hair off my forehead and gently tucked it behind my ear.

"Kelly?" I asked. I had heard of that name before.

"No, sweetheart, Callie—after your great-grandmother. You'll get to see her soon. She's so precious. We've all been taking turns holding her downstairs." Mom continued to caress my head and my arm. Her touch was a medicine more powerful than whatever was hanging in the bags above my head. I laid my head back and tried not to think of the baby.

"Ann will be here soon, too," she continued.

I smiled, thinking of my little sister, nearly nine years younger than me.

"She's been helping us watch the boys at home. Conner and Casen have missed you so much."

Conner and Casen. The little boys in the photos. I glanced off to the left, but the images were still blurry. It was all so confusing. I closed my eyes and tried not to let the fear I felt inside spill out. With every visitor had come new bits of information that seemed obvious to them but earth-shattering to me. Yet I had neither the strength nor the clarity to process it or to ask more questions.

"Mrs. Perkins, your other daughter is here," chirped one of the nurses from the door.

Mom squeezed my hand once more. "I'm going to go check on Callie downstairs, but I'll be back soon. You two have a nice visit."

She gently rose to her feet, picked up her purse, and walked toward the door. I immediately missed her touch.

As soon as Mom left, the nurse poked her head back into the doorway.

"Marcy, your sister is here to see you."

I looked toward the door, expecting a nine-year-old little girl to walk in holding Dad's hand. Instead, a grown woman with dark brown hair gathered up in a large, coiffed ponytail sauntered in. She was wearing a pink and purple tracksuit. She walked over to the edge of my bed and sat where Mom had been moments ago.

"Marcy!" She beamed as she reached for my hand. "Oh, I'm so glad to see your eyes open."

"Ann?" I turned my head slightly on the pillow to better examine her face. She was wearing pink lip gloss. Her eyes were unmistakably Ann's—large, bright, hazel, and doe-like. I would have recognized them anywhere. But . . . she was a woman in her twenties.

She tucked a piece of hair behind her ear. "Marcy, we've all been so worried about you. As soon as I heard the news, I jumped on a plane. Dad didn't want me to miss my midterms, but I couldn't stay away from my big sister."

Midterms? Ann is in college?

"We've been praying for you for days," she continued. "David and Marilynn Chadwick and so many other people from yours and Dev's church . . ."

More names I didn't recognize.

"They've all been here, praying over you. And then Mom got a call a couple of days ago from Bettye in Dallas. Remember Bettye Wideman?"

With a bit of relief, I realized I did remember Bettye. She had been a friend of our family's since I was a baby.

Ann didn't pause for me to answer, which was fine by me. "God gave her the verse John 11:4."

John 11:4. That I recognized. It was from the Bible. The New Testament. I just couldn't remember the words.

"Marcy, it was the same verse that God had given your pastor, David Chadwick. That's when I knew God would heal you. That this was not your time."

"John 11:4?" I asked, the words burning in my throat. I wanted to know what God might have been saying to other people that had had such a powerful effect on them—and on me.

"It's the story of Lazarus," she explained. "When Jesus hears that Lazarus is sick, he says, 'This sickness will not end in death. No, it is for God's glory.' That's when David knew you would come out of the coma. He told us all that this wasn't your time."

This sickness will not end in death . . . The story came into focus a bit. I kept rolling around the words that Jesus had spoken when Mary and Martha pleaded with him to heal their brother. But Lazarus died . . . did I die, too?

My mind was swirling, trying to figure out what the verse meant when Ann's voice brought me back to the room.

"Marcy, Callie's so beautiful. I've just come from rocking her awhile. I knew Dev needed help with Conner and Casen at home, but I've tried to be here as much as possible." Then her voice broke. "I just couldn't imagine my life without you."

She held my face in her hands, and I kept peering into her eyes. This was definitely Ann, but it was so strange seeing her as a grown woman. How could I have so completely forgotten the years that had passed?

We sat for a while in silence, Ann holding my hand, until one of the nurses came to the door and nodded that it was time for her to leave.

"Marcy, I'm so sorry I have to leave you," she said, "but I've got to go back to school. Midterms are this week, and I promised Dad." She stood and adjusted her purse on her shoulder. "Dev will be back soon, though, and you'll be able to see the kids again before you know it. Conner and Casen will be so excited to see you. They've missed you so much."

She leaned over and kissed my forehead. "I'm so glad you're okay. I love you."

I love you, too.

Once Ann was gone, I looked again at the photos taped to my bed. Dev, Mom, and Ann all seemed confident I was a mother of three children all under the age of six. Yet I couldn't even remember my wedding day. Was I ready to meet them? Ready to be a mom?

It seemed like—whether I was ready or not—I was going to meet them very soon.

CHAPTER 4

A SONG
FROM HEAVEN

"Marcy. Marcy, honey," a low, soft voice close to my ear said. "I'm back."

My eyes fluttered open, and I turned slightly to the right to see Dev sitting in the chair next to the bed.

"How are you feeling?" He seemed more cheerful than before, like a burden had been lifted from his shoulders. Like seeing me awake had somehow brought him to life too.

I swallowed and smiled weakly, still too tired to speak.

"Marcy, I have good news." He smiled. "The doctors say the antibiotics seem to be working. They think we'll be able to move you out of the ICU and into a private room soon. You'll be more comfortable there, and you'll be able to have more visitors." He brushed a stray hair off my forehead. "Conner and Casen can't wait to see you."

Conner and Casen. The little boys. *Our* little boys.

He stood and walked to the left side of the bed. "Have the photos helped?"

I swallowed hard. "They . . . I . . . they look a little blurry to me."

"That's okay . . . I know you're still tired." He reached for the photo taped farthest away and pulled it down. "Why don't we look at them together?"

He brought the photo to within a few inches of my face. I strained to focus, but my temples throbbed mercilessly.

"Here's Casen—our oldest. He's six now."

I blinked several times, focusing in on a photo of a small boy with sandy blond hair, wearing a green V-neck and shorts with white socks pulled up to his knees. He was beaming at the photographer.

Gosh, what a precious child . . . he looks so happy. And he has the same hair color as Dev.

"That was after the big soccer game last October. Casen scored two goals that day. I yelled so much, I went home with a sore throat." Dev laughed.

I studied the little boy's bright eyes, his big smile, how proud he looked in his uniform. I glanced up at Dev, his eyes so expectant. I didn't want to alarm him by indicating that I had no memory of this child, so I smiled and nodded.

Dev carefully stuck the picture back up on the bed. Then he untaped the next one. "And here's Conner—our rough-and-tumble toddler."

I squinted again as Dev held the photo up to my face. Another boy with sandy blond hair. But this one had dark, deep-set eyes and a darling dimple on his left cheek. In the photo, he appeared to be running down a long hallway, wearing white tennis shoes and a navy blue romper.

"This was from Easter weekend, about a year after we moved to Charlotte. He was looking for his basket."

"And this one . . . " Dev said as he pulled another photo down. "Your sister got this developed at the one-hour photo booth a few days ago. Honey, look at our beautiful baby girl."

I squinted to get a better view of the photo Dev was holding up. As my eyes adjusted, I could make out a woman in a white hospital gown with plastic bands around her wrist, smiling at the camera as she held a tiny, reddish . . . blur.

Why can't I see what's in the woman's hands? There must be something wrong with my eyes. Dev said it was a baby, but it just looks like a red splotch to me.

"And here, honey. This was when the boys came to see you and Callie after the delivery."

Dev held up another photo and watched my face as I squinted to see the details. The two boys were wearing turtlenecks and sweatshirts. The older boy was sitting in a blue chair, beaming as he delicately held a tiny baby swaddled in white blankets. The baby's eyes were closed, and her hands were folded on top of the blankets. The younger boy was standing next to the chair with one hand holding the arm of the chair and the other reaching for a woman kneeling next to him. She had dark, shoulder-length hair and was smiling wide at the camera. She was wearing a light pink nightgown and stud earrings. Her makeup was flawless, and her nails were painted light pink. She looked so happy. So full of life and joy. She looked just like . . .

Ann! This must be Ann's family. That's strange. Ann didn't mention having any kids.

"This was taken shortly after you gave birth to Callie, a few days ago. Before you got really sick."

That's me? I look so . . . old.

My head spun as I tried to piece together the different photos. The children were precious. But it was like watching a slideshow of someone else's life. The family was picture-perfect . . . I just didn't recognize it as mine.

"I know it's hard right now," Dev said. "This must all be pretty overwhelming. But I'm going to leave these photos right here," he said, taping them back up, "to help you remember."

"How . . ." I croaked, my throat still burning, "how are they?"

That seemed like the right thing to ask. What a concerned mom would ask.

Dev smiled. "Good, all things considered. We've had so much help. Your mom and dad came up from Texas as soon as they could to watch the boys. And friends have been stopping by day and night to drop off meals and run errands. Honestly, I think they barely know what's going on."

Well, that's a relief.

"And . . . the baby? How is she?"

"Callie's downstairs. We thought it best to leave her at the hospital. Dr. Bryan, our pediatrician . . . he's made sure that she's being taken care of."

Dev gently walked back to the chair on the other side of the bed. "Marcy, do you remember the elders from Forest Hill Church coming to lay hands on you and pray?"

I shook my head.

"The doctors let five of them come into the room to pray over you. It was so powerful. You could just feel that God was with us. The doctors said it would take a miracle for you to come out of that coma, but by the time we finished praying, I knew you were going to make it."

Wait . . . I remembered . . . something. But what?

"In fact," Dev continued, "David Chadwick was out of town in Kansas City. When he called Marilynn—his wife—from the airport and heard that you weren't responding to the medicines, he hurried to the hospital and prayed Lamentations 3:22-23 over you."

I raised my head a bit. "Which one is that?"

Dev smiled. "Let me see if I can remember it . . ." He closed his eyes. "Because of the LORD's great love we are not consumed, for his compassions never fail. They are new every morning; great is your faithfulness."

I laid my head back again. It was a beautiful verse. *Was that what I remembered?*

"When David was finished praying, he told us all you were going to come out of the coma the next morning. That God had said it was not your time. Four hours later, I got the call that you were waking up." Dev beamed. "The doctors agreed that there was no medical reason for you to recover."

Dev continued, "Earlier in the week, Marilynn thought music would be soothing, so she brought a tape recorder in, and they left some praise music playing in the corner. Do you remember?"

Yes . . . music! I remembered music!

I couldn't even begin to tell Dev about the music I had heard—whether it was a dream or a blip in my brain during the coma or something more miraculous—I had no idea. All I knew for sure was that it felt far more real than anything I had woken up to.

It sounded like a throng of voices so vast in number they couldn't be counted. The sound they made was heavenly and strange . . . almost haunting. It was like no music I had ever heard before, yet it felt as though it had been playing since the beginning of time. I never wanted it to end.

The voices were repeating one command over and over:

PRAISE THE LORD, PRAISE THE LORD, PRAISE THE LORD

It was a simple three-note melody, repeated over and over. The singing radiated from every direction at once, completely enveloping me in warmth, as if I were being carried along by the hand of the Lord, floating in the air without effort, soaring high above the ground, never feeling tired or growing weary.

PRAISE THE LORD, PRAISE THE LORD, PRAISE THE LORD

When I looked down, I saw what appeared to be hospital corridors. I floated through them like a dove on a breeze. Then I saw what appeared to be a crib. There was nothing in it—just blankets and a mattress—but for some reason I couldn't look away. I kept hovering above the crib, willing myself to descend, so I could look beneath the blankets. But no matter how hard I tried, I couldn't get myself to go lower. I couldn't land.

Then, I heard a second set of voices, separate from the choir. They were faint, as though they were off in the distance. Unlike the choir, their words did not form a discernible chorus—just a clatter of men's and women's voices talking over one another. They sounded rushed and jumbled. I couldn't understand what they were saying, but the noise seemed to be coming from the halls and rooms below me.

Then the singing grew louder—almost as if the choir was trying to drown the other voices out. And why wouldn't they? The singing was so beautiful. I could have listened to it forever.

"Marcy?" Dev's voice jerked me back to the hospital bed.

Had it been a dream? An effect of the medicines? A doorway between this life and the next?

"Yes . . ." I swallowed. "I remember the music."

I wanted it to come back. I wanted to soar freely again—not be trapped in this bed, my hands strapped down, covered in tubes. In the dream I had felt strong and alive. Here I just felt weak and lifeless, like I had fallen into a pit.

"When you came out of the coma, you asked the nurses to turn the music down. Do you remember that?"

The angelic music had been loud, so much so that it rang in my ears, drowning out everything and everyone else. I didn't remember talking to the nurses, but the music must have been loud if I had struggled to make the request with the way my throat was hurting.

"The praise music was on low, so we couldn't figure out why you thought it was so loud, but it seemed to help you."

Yes, I lamented, unable to hear anything now but the incessant beeping of the machine on my right, *it did.*

"All of the doctors working on your case agree that it's a miracle you're here," said Dev, his eyes glistening. "There's just no other reason to explain why you came out of the coma. The Lord has been with you the whole time."

I looked at Dev. That was the first thing anyone had said to me that made sense. God had been with me—always.

Before I left for college at SMU, I was sitting on my bed and my mom came in with a Bible in her hand. She sat next to me and opened it to a page she had bookmarked. I looked down and saw that she had underlined and dated Proverbs 3:5-6. I read the verse aloud: "Trust in the Lord with all your heart and do not lean on your own understanding. In all your ways acknowledge Him, and He will make your paths straight."

The night before I headed off on my own to college, God asked me to trust him with my life. To trust his paths instead of my own. I did then. So why couldn't I do it now? *Because now I have children— three children—with this sweet man I don't remember marrying. How can this be my life?*

It all felt so overwhelming. Here I was surrounded by all of these people, and yet I felt utterly and completely alone. I closed my eyes and swallowed hard. The faint strains of the mystical chorus I had heard once before echoed in my mind.

PRAISE THE LORD, PRAISE THE LORD, PRAISE THE LORD

I'm not alone. As soon as Dev mentioned the Lord, I knew in my depths, I'd never been alone.

The Lord is with me. Even here. In this lonely room. In this mess. And somehow, he's going to get me out of it.

CHAPTER 5

THE FACE
IN THE MIRROR

I opened my eyes. The pain lingered around my temples and neck like an unwelcome guest. But it had eased a bit, like Mom's touch had scared it off for a while.

The room was brighter than I remembered. A sliver of sunlight from the window behind me fell across the white bedsheets, which were pulled tight and clean across me. The antiseptic smell that had nauseated me had been replaced by the faint whiff of soap. I glanced off to my left. The photos that Dev had brought were still taped to the side rail. An IV bag hung to the right, but the Velcro straps that had held my wrists to the bed rails were gone.

Finally.

I looked up at the wall. The clock was gone, and in its place was a small black television. Just past the foot of the bed, in a small alcove, were a sink and a mirror, and just to the left of that, an open door to a small bathroom.

This must be the private room Dev mentioned. Maybe I really am getting better.

I wriggled my fingers a bit. With the Velcro straps gone, I could finally raise my arms. They felt leaden and slow, but at least it felt like a part of my body was back.

"It's good to see you awake, darling." Mom peered in from the doorway, carrying a bouquet of white roses and a toiletry bag. She set them down near the sink before coming over and kissing my forehead. The pain in my head eased slightly. I gingerly reached up and ran my fingers through my hair. It felt a bit oily and limp.

Gosh, I need a shampoo.

Then I felt it: the front right side of my head was prickly with stubble. I inhaled sharply.

"Mom, what did they do to my hair?"

She smiled as she adjusted some of the pieces that had fallen to the side. "The nurses had to shave a section off when the doctors relieved the pressure on your brain."

"Oh, no," I moaned.

"Don't worry, Marcy," Mom said reassuringly. "It will grow back soon enough. And I can help you fix it up."

Gosh . . . I must look terrible. I looked up at the mirror above the sink at the end of the bed, but the reflection looked blurry from several feet away. "I want to see. Can you help me get up?"

Mom pursed her lips. "Let's not worry about that right now. You need to rest. The important thing is that you recover your strength, so we can take you home."

"Mom, my head is shaved!" I sounded like a teenager pleading to stay out past curfew. "Please, just . . . help me get out of the bed."

"Okay . . ." Mom relented. "Let me get a nurse."

I needed to know what I looked like . . . to see how bad the damage was. To see if the person in the mirror looked as bad as I felt.

A few minutes later, Mom and a nurse returned through the doorway.

"I hear you want to see yourself," the nurse chirped happily. "Let's try to get you up."

She came to the bedside and pushed down on a small clasp to unlatch the bed rail. I sat up and slowly stretched my legs. It felt like years since I had been able to sit up. My head pounded, I felt woozy, and for a second, I thought I might pass out.

The nurse put her hands on my shins and slowly pulled my legs to the side of the bed. As I moved, a sharp pain jolted across my collarbone. I looked down to see a needle taped to the top of my chest connected to a thin clear tube that snaked across the bed rail to the bag hanging from the pole next to the bed.

"Be careful," the nurse said. "You don't want to pull out your PICC line." She nodded at the needle.

My what? I didn't even care. I just wanted to get to the mirror, no matter what it took.

"Marcy," Mom said, steadying me with her hand, "be careful, darling. Just take it slow."

I let my legs drop over the edge of the bed until my bare feet hit the cold linoleum floor. I tried to pull myself up, but my legs wobbled, and the nurse had to grab my shoulders to keep me from falling back onto the bed.

With one arm hitched onto the nurse's shoulder, I put my other hand on the IV pole to steady myself and took a few shuffling steps. Suddenly the cool, sterile air hit my backside.

Oh great . . . as if this isn't humiliating enough.

The nurse guided me to the edge of the sink with Mom trailing closely behind, her hands out just in case I tottered backward. Wheezing from the effort, I put my hands on the sides of the sink to steady myself and inhaled deeply before looking up into the mirror.

The face of the woman looking back at me was a sickly pale, like all the life had been sucked out of her. Lines and creases ran across her sunken cheeks. Dark, puffy bags hung under her eyes like bruises. Her hair—what remained of it—looked limp and dull. On her bottom lip was a fever blister the size of a dime.

I was horrified. I couldn't remember ever looking this bad. Or . . . this old.

How can I look this old?

Clearly I was not seventeen.

Wow, I'm in bad shape.

I reached up to my scalp again and moved a large flap of hair from one side to the other in an attempt to cover the patch that had been shaved.

"One of the nurses did that, darling," Mom explained. "So we could hide the bald spot. Wasn't that nice of her?"

Why was Mom trying to make everything better when it clearly wasn't?

"But Mom . . . my hair looks terrible."

"It's not so bad," she offered. "We can wash it soon and fix it up."

I met her eyes in the mirror. "Washing it isn't going to fix it. My head is *shaved*."

"I know, honey. But the important thing is that you are here with us." She gently rubbed my arms.

I stared in the mirror for a long time, trying to accept the truth of what it revealed—my hair, my age—all of it.

"Let's just get you back to bed," she finally said, calling the nurse back over.

Once again, the nurse gave me her shoulder, and with my other hand I grabbed the IV pole to steady myself. Just taking the ten short steps back to the bed drained me of what little energy I had. My body longed for rest. I closed my eyes, but all I could see were the faces of the three children from the photos taped to the bed. The beaming sandy blond boy after his big win. The bounding toddler looking for his Easter basket. And the tiny girl, so new in the world, being held by what I now realized was me, just days ago.

Will I remember them once I see them? Will it all come flooding back? Surely some kind of instinct will kick in once I see them . . . but what if it doesn't?

The ray of light from the window behind the bed slowly moved across the room as the hours went by, extending a shadow until the room grew dark.

~

I woke up to the sound of a small steel cart clanking across the room. The nurse's sneakers squeaked as she pushed the cart to the side of the bed next to the IV pole. Mom was sitting in a chair on the opposite side, flipping through a magazine.

"How are you feeling, Marcy?"

I cleared my throat to answer the nurse. "I'm . . . okay," I stammered. "I look awful. But I feel better than I did in the other room."

She nodded. "I'll bet you do! I just need to flush your PICC line," she said, nodding at the needle under my collarbone. "We don't want it to get infected."

Working quickly, she put her hands on my shoulders and tilted my torso up from the back. She rolled down the thin fabric right above my collarbone to where the clear tube snaked up to the IV bag.

I swallowed, suddenly feeling parched.

"This will sting a bit," she said as she took a syringe from the cart and began drawing clear liquid from a small vial. Once the syringe was full, she held it up in the air and flicked it with her fingers. Then she reached for the tube taped to the top of my collarbone and inserted the needle into the top plastic cap. As the clear liquid went into the tube, a hot burning entered my veins, spreading like wildfire across my chest.

"Ohhhhhhhh! That burns!"

"I know . . ." she said sympathetically, "we're almost done."

My palms got clammy as she continued to push the syringe. When she finally pulled the syringe away, the flames licking my chest cooled down, and I tried to catch my breath.

"Okay?" she asked hopefully.

I nodded, but I was not okay. *When is this nightmare going to end?*

"Another nurse will come sit with you tonight," she said to both my mother and me, "just in case you need anything." Then she smiled at me, and despite the pain, I smiled back.

"Thank you for everything," Mom said. Then, as soon as the nurse left, she set her magazine down and turned to me.

"Now that you're awake, let's work on your hair." She reached down into her bag and came back up with an aerosol can, a comb, a hand towel, and a small compact mirror. "I brought this dry shampoo from home. You'll look great in no time."

Dry shampoo doesn't make hair grow back, I lamented. Then again, maybe a shampoo *would* make me feel more human.

As I lifted myself into a sitting position, pain flickering across my chest, Mom placed the towel around my neck and started running the comb through what hair I had left. I hated feeling so helpless. And yet, Mom's touch felt so good.

She worked in small batches, taking one section of hair at a time and spraying it with a floral-scented mist. As she ran the comb through my hair, I thought about Dev's last visit and found myself wishing he would come back.

It felt weird to miss someone I didn't really know, but for some inexplicable reason, when he was in the room, I felt safe.

"Will Dev be back soon?" I asked.

"Of course. He just needs a good night's sleep," Mom said, tilting my head down so she could work on the back. "He's been up for days, calling friends all over the country to give them updates on you."

I couldn't even imagine how he must have felt. Almost losing someone he loved. All the doctors telling him there was little hope. *And with three small children. This must have been so hard for him.*

As Mom started working on the side of my head with the bald spot, I looked into the small mirror she had handed me, but when I did, I saw something much worse than my reflection.

Bright, sickly green and orange spots covered the mirror and everything around it. With horror, I looked around to find similar splotches covering the bedsheets and the ceilings as though someone had taken cans of paint and splattered their contents on every surface. Suddenly, the spots started to swirl, and my stomach churned.

"Mom, do you see the spots?" I said, unable to keep the panic from my voice. "They're all over the place!"

Mom put down the comb and looked around the room, her brow furrowed.

"Honey, I don't see any spots. Where do you see them?"

"They're everywhere . . . on the walls and ceilings." I looked down. "They're all over my arms!"

"Marcy, honey, are you feeling okay?" she said.

Suddenly a spot darted near my face. I reached out to grab it, but it disappeared into thin air.

"What are you doing?"

"I just feel so strange, Mom. I think there's something wrong with my eyes." Panic bubbled up. "Or maybe my brain."

I glanced back at the mirror. Staring back at me were not one but three faces—three women with gaunt cheeks, dark bruises under their eyes, and partially shaved heads.

"Mom, something's wrong," I said, no longer able to disguise the fear in my voice.

"Okay, let me get the nurse." She set the comb down and rushed out the door.

They said I'm getting better . . . but this feels worse!

I laid my head back and closed my eyes, terrified by what else I might see, but even in the darkness, my mind tormented me.

Three kids . . . Dev . . . a new baby downstairs . . . you fell into a coma . . . a hole in your skull . . . your husband is here . . . PRAISE THE LORD PRAISE THE LORD . . . the baby's not in the crib . . . turn the music down . . . patient goes by the name Marcy . . . I have to get back for my midterms . . . Conner and Casen and Callie . . . the boys will be here soon . . . they miss their mommy . . .

"Marcy," the nurse's voice broke through. "Your mother tells us you're seeing things." Mom was standing next to her smiling weakly at me.

"Yes. There's something wrong with my eyes," I said, relieved to see only one nurse standing there. "I'm seeing bright green and orange spots all over the room."

"Well," she said, looking at her clipboard, "you're on an awful lot of antibiotics and other medications. And hallucinations are common when there's swelling on the brain. They should go away soon, though."

But what if there's something really wrong with my brain . . . and it doesn't get better? I couldn't even bear to ask her for fear that her answer might be even more frightening than the question.

An agitation gripped my body. Every limb felt uncomfortable and keyed up like I needed to move. To get up. To get going.

"I want to leave," I said, fiddling with the clear tube on my chest.

"Marcy," the nurse said, reaching for my hands, "leave your IV line where it is."

I tried to swing my legs over the side of the bed, and the metal pole holding the bag teetered. Mom reached over to steady it.

"No, honey," she said, "you need to stay in bed." She turned to the nurse. "I hate to interrupt his sleep, but should I call Dev to come back to sit with her?"

"Yes!" I pleaded with her. "Please . . . call Dev."

I lay my head back on the pillow and closed my eyes. When I woke, Dev was standing in the doorway, wearing a T-shirt and khakis.

He looked concerned. "Your mom called to say you wanted me to come sit with you. She said you were seeing things."

"Dev . . ." I started to tear up. "I keep seeing spots. I think something is really wrong with my brain."

He walked over to the bed and reached for my hand.

"I'm so sorry," he said, sitting down. "I spoke to one of the doctors, and he said it's probably a combination of the medication and the swelling on your brain, but the antibiotics are working, and the swelling is going down. You just have to give it some time."

"But . . . what if my brain is always messed up like this?"

Dev gripped the bed rail firmly. "It won't be. You just have to be patient and let the medication work. The kids and I . . ." His eyes started to tear up. "We all want you to come home. We need you, Marcy. The boys need you; Callie needs you." He squeezed my hand. "And I need you."

He leaned over and kissed my forehead. "Try to get some rest."

"I've tried to sleep—I *want* to sleep—" I fought back a lump in my throat—"but every time I close my eyes, my brain starts racing."

He sat back for a second, then said, "Would it help if I lay down beside you?"

I considered it for a moment. For whatever reason, I did feel safer when he was in the room. Just him being here now made me feel better. I studied his face. He looked exhausted, yet there was a warmth in his eyes and a tenderness in his expression that was so comforting, so . . . *familiar.*

I nodded and moved over a bit.

He slipped off his shoes and lined them up at the foot of the bed. Then he lay down on his side, facing me, and put his arm around my waist. His touch felt . . . like it had been there before. Like my body, as beat up as it was, somehow remembered it from some time ago.

"Everything's going to be okay," he said softly. "I'm not going anywhere."

I lay my head back and tried to take deep breaths.

"If the spots come back," he said, "we'll chase them away together."

"But what if I fall asleep again and my mind keeps racing?"

"Then we'll stay up talking." Dev smiled softly and pulled me closer. "You can tell me anything you want."

Should I tell him that my memory hasn't come back yet? That I still don't remember our marriage, or our kids? Or that I'm terrified that I never will?

Dev closed his eyes, and before long, he was snoring softly, his arm going limp on my waist.

I watched him sleep. *God,* I silently prayed, *I feel so safe with this man. Even though I've only known him for a few days, I feel like I can trust him completely. I don't want him to leave my side. Everyone says it is a miracle I am still here. There must be a reason you brought me back. If it's to be with Dev and the children—our children—please . . . help me remember them. Help me get back to them.*

I closed my eyes, frightened that I would see the spots again, but instead I saw a football game. It was my freshman year of college at SMU. I was sitting in the bleachers wearing a brown shirt, and a friend introduced me to a handsome guy from Jacksonville, Texas. He had long blond hair and blue eyes. He shook my hand, and instead of letting go, he let it linger for a second, and my heart fluttered.

It felt both old and new, like it had happened in another lifetime and only a few moments ago.

Then I had another image. The same boy with long blond hair . . . talking about golf over a cup of frozen yogurt. We were sitting outside an ice cream shop on a warm October day laughing uncontrollably, and I never wanted our time together to end.

I remembered running down the hallway of my dorm on that same October day and announcing to anyone who would listen, "That's the man I'm going to marry!"

I opened my eyes. I remembered.

Dev.

Dev was my college sweetheart. The man I thought I would marry.

"Dev?" I said softly.

He stirred and rolled onto his back. I looked over at him and studied his face in the shadows.

There *was* something familiar about the shape of his lips. The color of his hair. His eyes. His hair was much shorter now, and his face looked older and careworn, but it was the same man. Even though I couldn't remember a wedding, I knew Dev was my husband.

Trust in the Lord . . .

I rolled onto my back and looked up at the ceiling.

Lord, I don't know why I can't remember my wedding day, but I do know that this is the same Dev that I knew in college—the one that I was falling in love with. And even though I can't remember it, I believe that we have built a life together, that we've had three children together, and that he's never stopped loving me. I don't know what's wrong with me, why my memories aren't coming back the way the doctors said they would. But I do know this—wherever this man goes . . . I will go with him.

CHAPTER 6

THE GIFT OF INTUITION

"Marcy, your mom just called. They're heading over with the boys. And the nurse is going to bring Callie in from the nursery."

I rubbed the sleep from my eyes and sat up in bed. Dev was sitting in a chair a few feet from the bed with a newspaper folded on his lap. The smell of fresh coffee from the Styrofoam cup in his hand awakened my senses.

A sliver of light from the window fell across the rumpled bedsheets. With Dev by my side, I had made it through the night without any strange hallucinations. The few times I had woken up, I felt Dev's arm around my waist, and I was able to fall back asleep. The long night was over. Then it struck me.

They're heading over . . .

Our kids . . . they're going to be here any minute.

My heart raced as I thought about the two little boys and baby girl from the photos and tried to imagine them standing in front of me. What would it be like to see three children I had no recollection of giving birth to? Would I eventually recognize them and remember our lives together? Would I be able to be the same mom that they had known? That they needed?

I looked down at the four photos taped to the bed rail, desperately hoping that another look might trigger a sliver of a memory. After all . . . I remembered Dev. Maybe the doctors were right. Maybe the swelling *was* going down.

They're beautiful children . . . and I know they belong to me and Dev because he told me they do, and I believe he's telling me the truth. I studied the pictures more.

Nothing.

I wonder what the boys will remember?

"Dev?" I glanced up from the photos. "What do the boys know about . . . about what's happened to me at the hospital?"

Dev cleared his throat. "Well, Conner's too young to absorb what's going on, so we haven't told him anything. But your parents and I told Casen that Mommy has been sick and needed to stay in the hospital a bit longer after having Callie."

I looked down at the tube coming out of my chest. "Does he know *how* sick?"

"We didn't tell him the details . . . just that you needed to stay in the hospital to rest. We *did* tell him that you might look a little different . . . that you'd be in bed, that you'd be tired, and that you might have some tubes attached to you."

I thought about the face that stared back at me from the mirror. If my reflection was alarming to me, I couldn't imagine how it would look to two small children.

"Have Casen and Conner seemed . . . affected by everything going on?"

Dev took a sip from his coffee cup and smiled. "They're taking everything in stride, sweetie. Conner is a ball of energy, and Casen has been on his best behavior. And of course they love that their grandparents are here."

"Have they seemed . . . *scared* at all?"

"Not that I can tell," Dev said thoughtfully. "Of course, I've been at the hospital most of the time. But between your parents, Ann, and friends stopping by the house, they've been in good hands. And Christine has been coming by a lot as well."

"Christine?"

"Tinie—our housekeeper," he prompted me. "She's been amazing. She's been asking about you every day."

We have a housekeeper? I rubbed my forehead. What else about my life didn't I know?

I glanced down at the photos again and tried to imagine those two little boys bounding into the room. A jumble of nerves coursed through my chest, like the feeling I used to get before a big test in school.

Maybe the memories will come back when I see them in person.

I was just about to ask Dev if we should ask the nurses to remove the PICC line while the boys were here, so they wouldn't be frightened by it, when the door swung open and a doctor walked in.

"Well hello there, Marcy," he beamed. "It's so good to see you sitting up." I quickly glanced over at Dev, who once again came to my rescue.

"Dr. Bryan," Dev said, shaking the man's hand, "it's good to see you again. Thanks so much for taking such good care of Callie for us. I was just telling Marcy how lucky we are to have you." Dev caught my eye. "Hands down, the best pediatrician in the business."

Thank you, Dev.

Dr. Bryan laughed awkwardly. "Well, I just wanted to stop in and talk to you about Callie's condition."

I shot Dev a panicked look. Even though I couldn't remember Callie, it seemed my motherly instincts were still operating full force.

"What condition?" I asked both of them at once. Dev took a deep breath and sat down next to me on the bed.

"It's nothing serious," he said, taking my hand. "We didn't tell you right away because we didn't want to upset you. Callie's fine . . ." he continued, "she just has a little problem with her mouth."

I looked at the doctor, who quickly jumped in. "Marcy, Callie has what is called a soft cleft palate."

"What is that?" I asked, my eyes darting frantically between them.

"Take your tongue and touch the back of the roof of your mouth," Dr. Bryan said. "The soft spot—where it feels all smooth?"

I nodded.

"Well, Callie doesn't have that," he explained. "It just means that part of her mouth didn't close completely."

"Is she in pain?" I asked, half-terrified of the answer.

"No, not at all," he said. "But she may have some trouble feeding, and she is going to be very prone to ear infections. In fact, we're treating her for one right now. That's why we've kept her here in the hospital instead of sending her home. It's easier to monitor her here."

"Can you fix it?" I asked.

"Oh yes, we can definitely fix it," he said, sending a flood of relief through my veins. "We're going to have to wait a few months until she's a little bigger, but after that, she shouldn't have any problems."

Dev squeezed my hand. "See, sweetie? She's going to be just fine. You both are."

"Have you seen Callie yet?" Dr. Bryan asked.

"Not yet." Dev saved me the trouble of trying to speak over the lump of emotion that had risen in my throat. "Marcy's parents are bringing the boys by in a few minutes. We thought we'd wait until the whole family was here."

"Well—"the doctor smiled brightly at me—"I certainly don't want to get in the way of that. I just wanted to stop by. Marcy—"he leaned in and took both of my hands in his—"it's so good to see you up and awake. Now, don't you worry. Callie is going to be just fine."

"Thank you," I croaked, my eyes beginning to well up.

"Is she really okay?" I asked Dev after Dr. Bryan left.

"Sweetie, she's beautiful." He leaned in and kissed my forehead. "You both are."

Just then, the door swung open again.

"Marcy, some special visitors are here to see you." The nurse smiled widely. Soft voices echoed from out in the hallway. Seconds later, my mom stepped in, followed by a nurse pushing a rolling crib. I could see a tiny pink forehead peeking out at the top.

Right behind the nurse came my dad, who was wearing a freshly pressed striped button-down. Each of his hands rested on the shoulders of two sandy-haired boys wearing matching navy polo shirts and khaki shorts. The older boy glanced around the room hesitantly as he took a few steps in, looking toward the bed. The younger boy smiled widely at me, showing off that perfect dimple on his left cheek.

I sat up straighter and ran my fingers through my hair, making sure the bald spot was covered, and pulled the sheets up to hide the PICC line.

Dad walked over and kissed my forehead. "Hello, sweetheart." The boys stayed close to Mom, hiding behind her as she placed the car seat on the floor next to Dev.

"Conner, Casen," my mom said, "aren't you glad to see Mommy?" They both nodded as they assessed me from afar.

Mommy. It still sounded so strange. *Come on, Marcy,* I chided myself. *You can do this.*

"Hi, Conner! Hi, Casen! I'm so happy to see you!" I smiled brightly. Casen smiled back shyly, while Conner started to jump nervously from one foot to the other.

My gosh . . . what beautiful boys.

"Boys," Dev said, "can you go give your mom a hug?"

As soon as he said it, the boys ran to the side of my bed, reaching through the bed rail to grab my hands. Their little hands were warm and slightly sticky, and as soon as we touched, a wave of clarity came upon me.

These boys are mine. Conner and Casen are mine.

I didn't remember giving birth to them, rocking them to sleep, bathing them, or reading them bedtime stories. And I couldn't remember their first steps, their first birthdays, or their first words. But somehow I knew in my soul that Casen and Conner were my children.

It was like some invisible string hung between us that bound us together across time and space. It was a bond that nothing—not even a coma or memory loss—could erase. I couldn't explain it. I just knew. They were mine. And they always would be.

A single tear slid down my cheek as I took in this gift—a gift that had been given to me long ago, before I could remember. Before I forgot.

Trust in the Lord . . .

"Conner, Casen, why don't you come up on the bed?" I said, wiping away the tear. "So you can sit close to Mommy?"

They cautiously looked over at Dev, who nodded his approval. "Need some help, buddy?" he said and hoisted Conner up while Casen climbed up on his own. When they inched closer to me, I caught a whiff of their scent—an unmistakable blend of sun and dirt and mischief—a *boy* smell—further cementing the knowledge that yes, these were my boys.

I put my left arm around both of them and drew them in close, inhaling the moment as I kissed both of them on their foreheads.

Thank you, Lord . . . thank you for these children, and for confirming in my spirit that they are mine. Please help me get better so I can leave this place and be with them every moment of every day. They need me, Lord, and I need them.

"Callie's ready to see you too," said Mom. "Do you feel ready to hold her, Marcy?"

I was—now more than ever.

"Yes, please." I nodded.

Mom bent down and carefully gathered up Callie's tiny body from the blankets, cradling her head as Callie let out a soft cry. Mom had dressed her in a long white dress with a smocked yoke. As she walked toward me, beaming, Callie's features finally came into focus—her tiny button nose, pink lips, and delicate wisps of blonde hair.

When she laid that precious little bundle in my arms, the boys moved farther down on the bed, and the familiar new baby scent of soap and milk brought an immediate smile to my lips.

She was the prettiest baby I'd ever seen. Her tiny hands, her ears, her little nose, the way her mouth curled up at the sides. Everything about her was perfect.

I studied every part of this tiny creature who was mine and Dev's, and Callie stretched her arms out a bit, yawning widely. Every movement was a small miracle. I held her tiny hand in mine, and the feel of her smooth skin on mine sealed our bond. Dev walked over and put his hand on my shoulder.

"Isn't she beautiful, Marcy?"

"She's . . . wonderful," I said, my eyes misting as I tried to commit all her features to memory. I wanted to stay in bed all day holding her.

I'm so sorry that I wasn't able to be with you in your first days of life. I was so very sick. But now we're together, and I'm going to take care of you. I promise.

I looked up to see Dad sitting in the chair and Mom standing beside him, both looking at me and the kids with pride.

"See? You're a natural," said Mom. "Even after all you've been through, you know exactly what to do."

Dad nodded. "The boys have been so excited for you to come

home. I think they're getting a bit tired of playing in the yard with me."

"We finally got in touch with Jamey," Mom said.

I knew that name. My little brother. Well . . . probably not so little anymore.

"Where is he?" I asked, unable to pull my eyes off of Callie.

"He's still out of the country on assignment. We told him what you had been through," she said. "He's so thankful you're okay. He said to tell you he loves you and to give you a big hug, and that he'll call once you get home."

Part of me wanted to ask what "on assignment" meant. But I was so happy just being with the kids, I opted not to go down that path just yet.

"I can't wait to see him," I said, smiling. It *was* true after all. In fact, this was the first normal conversation I'd had since I woke up several days ago. And it felt wonderful.

I looked down at the boys. "Casen, Conner, can you tell Mommy what you've been doing while I've been gone?"

"Playing with Aunt Ann and riding my bike," Casen chirped.

Then Conner chimed in. "Playing cars!"

"It sounds like you've been having a lot of fun!" They were so adorable I could barely stand it.

Then a small wave of grief washed over me. I had no idea what Casen and Conner normally liked to do. What their favorite colors were. What their favorite books were. What foods they liked and disliked. What their favorite toys and games were. What scared them. What made them happy . . .

Please, Lord, let me remember these little boys' lives.

I looked down as Callie moved in my arms. "And what do you boys think of your new baby sister?"

Conner was already on the move, wiggling down to the end of the bed.

"I got to hold her!" said Casen. "When we came to visit you last time."

I shot Dev a panicked look.

"That's right, Casen," Dev said more to me than him. "You came to see Mommy right after she had Callie, didn't you?"

My pulse slowed a bit. They must have come to visit right after the delivery. My mind flashed to the picture of Ann holding a baby with two little boys. That wasn't Ann. It was me—right after I'd had Callie and before the infection and the coma.

I suddenly felt angry. *Everything I've lost. Surely the swelling has gone down by now. What if this is it? What if the rest of my life never comes back?*

I closed my eyes and pinched the bridge of my nose in frustration. No longer the center of attention, Conner started bouncing up and down on the bed like he was on a trampoline, and Casen started giggling and trying to grab his hands.

"Okay, time to settle down, boys," said Dev. "Let's sit next to Mommy quietly. She's been waiting to visit with you."

Dev came over and gently put his hands on each boy's shoulder, guiding them back up to me. Giggling, the boys collapsed into my one free arm. As their familiar boy smell washed over me again, a fresh determination welled up within me.

I'm going to do whatever it takes to go home with these boys as soon as I can. I had already lost too much time with them—time I might never get back. If my old memories *were* gone forever, I needed to start making new ones—now. And now that I knew how much Callie needed me, there was no way I was going to leave these kids without a mother again.

"Marcy?" a deep voice broke the spell. We all looked up. A male nurse I hadn't seen before rolled a wheelchair through the doorway. "I'm here to take you for your CT scan. Your doctor wants to check your sinuses to make sure the infection is clearing up."

I looked down at Callie, fast asleep in my arms and the boys curled up next to me.

You have got to be kidding me . . .

The kids and I had barely had fifteen minutes together. The last thing I needed was to be taken away from my family again.

I cleared my throat. "Do we have to do this right now? Could we at least wait until my kids leave?"

"I'm sorry," he said sheepishly. "They're waiting for you now."

I looked at Dev pleadingly. "Couldn't we reschedule the scan for later?" he asked, resting his hand on my shoulder as though he were trying to hold me in place.

"I'm sorry," the nurse repeated. "We have to go now."

Dev looked down at me, the disappointment in his eyes mirroring mine. "Okay, Casen, Conner, your mom needs to go to another room, so let's let her get up," he said.

"But I don't want Mommy to leave!" Casen wailed as he and Conner scrambled off the bed, startling Callie, who suddenly began to fuss.

Honestly, I lamented, *haven't we all been through enough?*

Mom leaned over and took Callie from me, quickly clearing a path for the wheelchair. Frustrated and determined to make this quick, I made the mistake of trying to stand on my own and instantly felt dizzy. I grabbed onto the IV pole with one hand to steady myself and dropped, more than sat, down into the wheelchair. I was so angry I could have screamed. Instead, I quickly collected myself, put on the biggest smile I could muster, leaned forward, and asked the boys, "Will you walk down the hall with me?"

The boys both nodded and grabbed onto Dev's hands, trailing behind me as I was wheeled out of the room and toward the elevator at the end of the hall, silently fuming the entire time.

I can't believe this. My boys have been away from me for so long, and now I have to leave them? Minutes after they arrive? This isn't right!

As the elevator grew closer, the trip I'd wished would go quickly suddenly seemed to be going too fast.

Once we were in the elevator, the nurse spun the chair around so I could see the boys. The gesture was at once welcome and cruel. Conner's face looked positively stricken.

"Mommy," he quietly called out. Before I could answer, the doors closed, and just like that, my boys had been taken away from me—again.

"Cute kids," the nurse said. "Don't worry. You'll be back with them before you know it."

My jaw clenched in raw determination. *You can bet on it.*

CHAPTER 7

ANXIOUS FOR HOME

"Good morning, Marcy! Are you ready to try some walking today?"

I turned and sat up in bed to see a large, affable man in a polo and sneakers standing at the door—my physical therapist. It wasn't the first time he'd come by—last time, I had struggled somewhat. But I was stronger now.

"I understand you've been asking the doctors about going home," he said.

He had *that* right. Every time someone came into the room to check my vitals, fluids, or even to bring me a meal, I grilled them on what I had to do in order to leave. It had been just over a week since I woke from my coma, and I was feeling a lot better. My throat was no longer raw, my vision had improved, and the dancing spots had not returned. Those boys had been without their mother long enough, poor Dev was exhausted trying to split his time between me here and the kids at home, and Callie was home now too, waiting for me. Besides, my memory didn't seem to be improving at all just lying around in this bed for days on end. Maybe if I got back home, the sights and sounds of my old life would start to trigger it.

"The scan we got yesterday looks good," he continued. "The infection is clearing, and the antibiotics seem to be working."

"So do you know when I'll be able to leave?" I asked.

"That's really up to the doctors. I'm just here to make sure you're regaining some strength."

That was a real concern. Just walking to the mirror had been a challenge. If I was going to have a prayer at keeping up with those two little boys *and* taking care of a newborn, I did need to build some stamina.

Dev was sitting in the chair next to the bed, watching a basketball game on mute. He stood up now. "Here, Marcy, let me get the robe that your mom brought from home," he said, grabbing a fluffy blue robe from the back of the bathroom door and wrapping me in it like a blanket.

"Thanks, sweetie." I quickly caught myself. *Sweetie? Is that right?* I glanced at Dev, and he smiled. *Must be.*

"Okay, let's get you out in the hallway." The physical therapist walked over and guided me with one hand while I tightly held onto the IV pole with the other.

The hallway was long, white, and lit by overhead fluorescent lights. Doors to other rooms lined both sides, serving as mile markers as I looked toward the exit sign down at the end.

That's the goal.

The physical therapist held up a long piece of blue fabric with a strap attached to the middle and secured it around my waist as Dev watched from the doorway. The belt was heavy, like a fanny pack filled with coins.

"Now, I'm holding onto the strap, so if you start to feel dizzy or weak, don't panic, I'll steady you. Okay?"

Do they really think I can't walk? I've been walking my whole life.

"I'll be okay," I assured him.

"Why don't you try taking a few steps toward the doors over there?"

I looked ahead to where he was pointing to two swinging doors about thirty feet away. They seemed close yet so far, like the finish line at the end of a marathon.

I steeled my gaze straight ahead and stepped forward with my right foot, then my left. The cold linoleum sent a chill through my leg. I could feel the therapist's firm grasp on the strap at my lower back. I took a deep breath.

You got this, Marcy . . . just a few more steps, a little faster now. Show them how easy it is. That you'll be fine at the house.

When I quickened my pace, however, I wobbled a bit, and the therapist tightened his grip on the strap.

"It's okay, Marcy, just take your time."

Just focus . . . you can do this. Walk toward the EXIT sign.

After several awkward seconds, I took a couple more steps. I tried to keep my head held high and my gaze forward, like a model on a runway, but I felt more like a fawn standing up for the first time.

I gritted my teeth, mustering what little energy I had left, and took several more steps. But as I lifted my leg for the last one, I started to tip back. The therapist quickly pulled on the strap and held his arms out to keep me from toppling over.

"That's probably good for now, Marcy," said the therapist. "You've been in bed for a while, so it makes sense that your legs are weak. We just need to build up your strength."

I sighed and looked up at Dev.

"It will get easier with time," Dev said as the therapist guided me back to the bed. I lay back on the pillow, totally spent.

It felt like the doctors were testing me—trying to see if I could make it outside of the hospital—and I had clearly failed.

—

Later that afternoon, a middle-aged woman arrived in the doorway, carrying a large folder. Mom, who had come earlier in the day so that Dev could go to his office, was needlepointing a Christmas stocking for Callie while *General Hospital* played on mute.

"Hello, Marcy. My name is Nancy. I'm your occupational therapist. I'm here to walk through a couple of simple exercises with you. Nothing too difficult—just a few basic skills you'll need to do every day." Nancy rolled a small table in front of me.

I wondered what that meant. Getting dressed? Changing Callie's diapers?

"The first thing we want you to do is write out a check."

Oh, I can do that.

She tore a check from a pad in her notebook and placed a pen in my hand. I looked down at the check with its blank lines, utterly and completely perplexed.

What's the matter with me? I scolded myself. *I've written out checks before.* But for the life of me, I had no idea what went on each line.

"Let's start with the date," Nancy said. "Today is April 9."

April 9 . . . April 9 . . . I stared blankly at the check as the therapist waited. *I know I know how to write a check. Mom taught me how to do this when I was a teenager.* I gripped the pen tighter and bit my lip. No matter how hard I tried to remember, I just couldn't figure out where to start the date.

"It's okay, Marcy," the therapist said. "Can you write out the name Jane Doe? Then make the check out for $150."

I glanced up at Mom. She was leaning forward in her seat, her eyes wide with expectancy. "You can do it, honey," she encouraged me. "Just write Jane Doe."

I knew I needed to start with a "J," but which line did it go on? And did I write out the numbers as words or numerals?

Sulking, I looked up at Mom, who was standing over my shoulder, glancing down at the table. She smiled, but her eyes were tight with worry.

"Can you write out 1-5-0?" Mom asked gently.

I looked down again at the check.

After several uncomfortable moments, the therapist put the check back in her folder without saying a word. I stared blankly ahead, hoping that she'd wrap up our session and let me get back in bed.

No such luck.

"Let's try something else, Marcy. I want you to address an envelope. Do you know how to do that?"

Of course I know how to address an envelope, I thought defiantly. *I've sent hundreds of letters before.*

I nodded politely, my pulse quickening with fear.

"I want you to make this envelope out to our current president, George H. W. Bush, and from yourself."

George H. W. Bush? Who is . . . ? Never mind that. I know how to spell George. G . . . E . . . O . . . Wait, where does the name go again? Does it go in the middle of the envelope, or the corner?

I looked up at Mom again, searching her face for a clue. She just looked concerned.

Please, Lord, help me pass this test. I have to show the hospital staff I'm well enough to go home.

"This is where the 'to' line goes," said the therapist, pointing down at the center.

"I'm having a bit of trouble remembering," I muttered.

"That's okay," she said. "Let's try to write your name in the upper left-hand corner. That's where the return name and address go."

I stared at the corner for several seconds.

I knew my name was Marcy . . . and if I was married to Dev, then I must have had his last name . . . but I couldn't remember what it was, let alone the street address for where we lived.

"Darling, I know you can write your name. It's Marcy Gregg . . . two g's at the end," Mom prompted.

It sounded simple enough, but I still couldn't seem to get my hands to form the letters.

After a few minutes of my staring at the envelope, the therapist pulled out another one and placed it on the table above mine.

"Here," she said, "try copying what's written on this envelope."

The new envelope had the words "George H. W. Bush" in large bold letters in the center, followed by some numbers and "Washington, DC." In the top-left corner was "Marcy Gregg," followed by more letters and numbers I didn't recognize.

I began slowly copying out the letters and numbers, looking back and forth between the two envelopes. I could feel the therapist's eyes on me and my pen. I could trace the shapes well enough, but taken together, the letters and numbers were more like squiggles than legible words.

"Maybe we should try again tomorrow," she said, taking the envelopes away.

"I know I can do it," I assured her. "I guess my head is still a little fuzzy from all the medication." I glanced up at Mom, who smiled at me sweetly and nodded. The therapist, however, looked slightly less convinced.

"The doctors are going to check on you tomorrow to see how you're progressing," she said, packing up her things. "Try to be patient, Marcy. Sometimes it takes a while to get everything back."

I didn't want to be patient. I didn't want to be *a* patient. I just wanted to go home and be with my kids. I didn't need to know how to address an envelope to take care of Callie or to play with Casen and Conner.

I could feel tears stinging the backs of my eyes.

As the therapist wheeled her little table out the door, Mom followed her, I hoped, to help plead my case. That's when reality hit.

Who was I kidding? I couldn't even walk down the hall without stumbling. Still . . . the physical strength I *knew* I'd get back. I just had to keep moving. But why wasn't my memory coming back? All the doctors agreed the antibiotics were working and the swelling had come down. So why couldn't I remember marrying Dev or having the kids? And why couldn't I write?

Panic started to bubble up. *What else have I forgotten how to do?*

I quickly wiped the tears from my cheeks. *Don't look helpless. If you look like you can't take care of yourself, they'll never let you leave.* I took a deep breath. *You can do this. Walking faster so you can keep up with the kids will come. And once you're back home, surrounded by all of your things, the memories will come back too. As for the other stuff . . . well, Dev can help with the checks and the mail and whatever else is still hazy until you're feeling 100 percent. You'll be fine.*

By the time Mom came back, I had convinced myself I had what it took to get out of here. Now I just had to convince everyone else.

CHAPTER 8

AUDITIONS FOR LIFE

Dev hung up the phone on the table next to my bed. "Marcy, do you feel up for a visitor this afternoon?"

I nodded, even though I felt weaker today than usual. I hoped that if I stayed upbeat and active, the hospital staff would believe I was well enough to go home. "Sure." I smiled. "Who's planning to visit now?"

The last two days had been a merry-go-round of neighbors, Dev's colleagues, and friends from church stopping by with flowers, cards, and assurances that they had been praying for my quick recovery. Every visitor was warm and caring; it was clear that Dev and I had a great network of friends in Charlotte. But each visitor was a stranger to me—a stranger who just happened to know more about my life than I did.

Each time someone came, Dev would fill me in on the details beforehand, so I would have context for the ensuing conversation.

He knew that my memory was still foggy, but he didn't know just *how* confused I actually was. Nor did he realize I didn't actually recognize any of the visitors. To him, they were longtime friends. But as far as I was concerned, they were simply the cast of a play I'd never seen.

"Holly," Dev informed me. "She's been checking in on you constantly."

Holly . . . I stared blankly at Dev, who took the cue that I needed a bit of help.

"She's a dear friend, one of our neighbors. She's called the house every few days to see how you're progressing."

"Of course," I said brightly, trying to gear myself up for another confusing conversation with a complete stranger who somehow knew me quite well.

Later that afternoon, an attractive blonde woman wearing a red pullover sweater showed up in the doorway holding an arrangement of hydrangeas. She smiled brightly as she shyly walked into the room.

"Hi, Holly!" Dev said, standing.

"Hi, Holly!" I parroted as she walked toward me. She set the hydrangeas on the table beside the bed and leaned over to give me a hug. As she pulled back, I racked my brain, trying to retrieve a sliver of memory that could give me some context for our friendship, but nothing came to mind.

"It's great to see you recovering so well, Marcy!" she said, smiling. "Everyone is asking how you're feeling and when you'll be able to come home."

"Oh, that's very sweet," I replied. "Soon, I hope."

"Yes, several neighbors have already dropped off meals this week," said Dev, gently prepping me for my next line.

"Well, that's wonderful. I hope to be home any day now," I said. "It will be so great to see you and . . . everyone else."

There was a brief pause in the conversation. I started to panic. I glanced at Dev, but he was busy fussing with the flowers Holly had brought. I was going to have to wing it.

"Gosh, Holly, did you have this much trouble when you had your children?" I asked.

Silence reverberated off the walls.

Holly glanced at Dev, who was looking at me like I had just spoken in another language.

My heart sank to the pit of my stomach. I could have sworn Dev mentioned that Holly had children. *Didn't he?*

Holly cleared her throat. "I adopted Madeline, Marcy. Don't you remember? You came over right after I got the call that she had been born."

My face burned with embarrassment as I glanced up at Dev again.

"Oh, of course! I just meant . . ." I swallowed. "Was it this difficult . . ." But I trailed off. There was no way to recover.

Seeing that I was flailing, Dev quickly chimed in. "I'm sure Marcy would love to hear some updates from the neighbors."

Holly paused a few seconds before telling me and Dev about a new family that had moved in a few houses down, but everything else she said during her visit passed over my head. I was too distracted to listen as I kept replaying my question over in my mind about her giving birth to her adopted daughter. It was a clear misstep that had proven I wasn't just confused; the memories were not coming back. By the time Holly left, I felt like crawling into a hole.

"I'm sorry, Dev," I said after she'd gone. "I don't know what I was thinking. It just slipped out."

He put his hand on my shoulder. There was kindness in his eyes, but it was mixed with a trace of worry, confirming my worst fears. He knew. Acting upbeat and chipper couldn't hide the fact that I didn't remember anything about our life together. And if I couldn't fool Dev, what chance did I have with the doctors?

I waited to see if Dev would probe further, but he just stood by the bed, gently massaging my shoulder until I closed my eyes in the fading light of the early evening. I was relieved by our mutual silence.

—

The next morning I awoke to a doctor I hadn't seen before standing in the doorway with a clipboard.

Dev was sitting nearby reading a newspaper while Mom chatted quietly into the phone. "I'll call back soon, Ann," she said as the doctor stepped into the room.

"Good morning! I'm Dr. Howell, one of the infectious disease doctors. I've been part of the team that's been watching your case closely."

"It's nice to meet you," I said, sitting up so I could pay attention.

"Thanks for all your work," Dev said as he folded the paper.

"You're welcome." He smiled at Dev then returned his focus to me. "So . . . we got the results back from your recent CT scan. The good news is that the infection in your brain appears to have cleared up faster than we had anticipated. It really is incredible that you came out of the coma and that your vitals have stabilized this quickly."

"That's great to hear," Dev said, taking my hand in his. "Does that mean Marcy can come home soon?"

"Well, that's what I'm here to discuss."

Please, Lord, let him have good news.

"Unfortunately, Marcy, you have been very sick, and it takes time to get better. The exercises you did with the physical therapist and the occupational therapist show some deficits. It's clear you're still physically weak. And you seem to be having some short-term memory issues. We just don't know if you're ready to face everyday activities around the house."

Dev put his other hand on my shoulder. I caught his eye and silently pleaded with him not to tell the doctor about my misstep with Holly yesterday. To his credit, he didn't say a word. Still . . . I knew he had to be thinking it.

"And your long-term recall doesn't seem to be coming back as quickly as we hoped either . . ."

I wasn't sure how they knew that, though there had been a steady stream of doctors and nurses through the room while friends and neighbors visited. I supposed it was possible they picked up on something. Maybe I wasn't as good an actress as I thought.

"We think that rehab might not be a bad idea," he said.

Rehab? My mind reeled. *They want me to do more exercises that make me feel like a child? That I can't possibly pass?*

I glanced up at Mom, whose eyes were tight with worry. "Where would Marcy go for that?" she asked.

"There's an excellent facility a few miles down the road. You could stay there for another week and work with therapists to regain your strength and some basic skills before you head home."

Another week in a facility? He had to be kidding. Didn't he realize I had three young children?

"No, I don't need rehab," I blurted out, more sharply than I expected. "I'm fine, really."

Dr. Howell looked at Mom and Dev, both of whom were fumbling for a response.

"Can't the hospital send a therapist to the house and work with me there?" I suggested.

"Yes," he conceded hesitantly, "we can certainly arrange for in-home care."

I looked up at Dev, who raised an eyebrow at me. I knew he was not going to make the decision for me. It was my call.

I glanced around the room, trying to imagine being sent to another lonely medical facility, away from the boys and Callie. Picturing myself trying to write out another check—and failing miserably—was beyond depressing and a bit embarrassing. Despite a niggling voice that wondered if perhaps the doctors might be right, it was clear what I had to do.

"I want to be with my family," I said. "Dev and my parents will be there to help until I'm back at full speed. Plus, we have . . ." I fumbled in my mind for the name of the nanny Dev had mentioned but came up blank. ". . . a nanny. She can help with the kids too. Really, I'll be fine."

Dr. Howell's eyes widened as he jotted down some notes. "Okay." He shook his head ever so slightly, a clear tell to his personal thoughts on the matter. "If that's what you want."

As he left the room, I looked at Dev for some assurance that I had made the right decision.

He smiled weakly at me, then started scanning the room. "Well, I guess we can pack up then," he said.

I looked at Mom. Surely, she had to support my decision. After all, she was a mother too.

"I'll stay as long as you need help, darling." She smiled, her eyes still carrying a trace of concern.

"Thanks, Mom," I said, taking her hand. "I know I'll feel better once I'm back in my own house."

Mom smiled weakly, then began tidying the room, throwing away empty cups and gathering up old magazines brought from the house.

The longer I sat watching Mom and Dev clean up, preparing for the big transition, the more the weight of my decision began to sink like lead into the pit of my stomach.

I had just signed up for the biggest acting gig of my life.

PART 2

THE SCENT OF MEMORY

CHAPTER 9

A
PERSUASION
OF PERFUME

I can't drink any more of this stuff.

The Ensure the nurses had given me on my last morning at the hospital felt like chalk in my throat. Somehow the hospital even managed to ruin chocolate. I couldn't get out of this place soon enough.

Mom had put me in a blue robe, dry-shampooed my hair, and applied some blush to brighten my pale skin before a nurse rolled me down to the lobby to wait for Dev. I grimaced as I forced another sip. I had no idea what kind of a cook I was, but I was fairly confident I could pull together something better than this.

As Dev slowly pulled the car around, the jumble of nerves that had kept me awake last night tightened in my chest. I was beyond relieved not to be going to some rehab facility, and I couldn't wait to be with the kids every day—to hold Callie and play with Conner and Casen, but I was still nervous about what lay ahead. What if

I couldn't find my way around the house? The kitchen? What if I couldn't remember how to make the boys' favorite meals, or even what they were? Where did I normally sit at dinnertime? Eventually, Dev was going to have to go back to work full time. How would I respond to phone calls and visits from people I couldn't remember without him there to prompt me first? My legs were still weak. What if we had stairs? Would I even be able to climb them?

These and other anxieties swirled as Dev pulled out of the parking lot and onto a four-lane road.

"Wait until you see what the neighbors have done for you." Dev smiled.

"What?" I asked, trying to stave off any unnecessary surprises.

"When I told them you were coming home today, they decorated the whole front of the house with balloons and a banner. They can't wait to see you."

My throat started to constrict. I was already nervous enough. The thought of arriving home—to a house I didn't know—and being greeted by hordes of people I couldn't remember all asking me questions I wouldn't be able to answer was more than I could handle. I forced a smile at Dev and then quickly turned to look out the passenger-side window, taking long, slow deep breaths in an attempt to calm myself down.

Please, Lord, tell me I haven't just made a colossal mistake.

I had to admit, the streets of suburban Charlotte were idyllic in the afternoon sun, with bright, colorful gardens and kids playing in the front yards—definitely an improvement over the cold, colorless, sterile environment of the hospital.

Eventually, Dev turned onto a quiet street lined with brick ranch homes and pulled into a sloped driveway.

"Welcome home, Marcy." He smiled.

I peered up at the house . . . our house.

As Dev unloaded the back of the station wagon, I stayed in my seat and took in as many details as possible. It was a red-brick, one-story ranch with a wide front porch flanked by perfectly manicured bushes. The door and shutters were a deep blue-green, much darker than the lawn. Balloons and a big handmade "Welcome Home, Marcy" sign hung over the porch, just like Dev had said, but thankfully, there was not a neighbor in sight.

"Here, give me your arm," Dev said as he opened the passenger door. I grabbed onto his arm and gingerly pushed myself up from the seat, my legs still a little wobbly. But the fresh air that filled my lungs felt absolutely heavenly.

"I can't even keep track of how many friends have stopped by with meals," Dev said, closing the car door behind me.

Gosh, I thought, *if he can't keep track of them, how will I?*

As we slowly made our way up the winding path to the porch, two small, beaming faces appeared through the glass pane of the front door. Mom and Dad appeared behind the boys a few seconds later, and Dad swung the door open. "Look who's finally home!" he announced as Casen and Conner spilled out onto the porch like a couple of unleashed puppies.

"Mommy!" they cried, racing across the lawn. Dev tried to slow them down, but he was unable to stop them before they each grabbed hold of one of my legs, nearly knocking me down.

"Whoa . . . easy there, boys," Dev said, steadying me with his one free hand. "Mommy's still a little tired. Let's not wear her out before she even gets inside."

Frankly, I couldn't have asked for a better welcoming committee.

"I missed you two so much," I said, reaching down and running my fingers through their hair. Even though it had only been a couple of days, it felt like weeks since the boys had visited me in the hospital.

"Where's Callie?" I asked Dad.

"Your mother's got her," he said, craning his neck back toward the house. I glanced over his shoulder to see Mom coming down the front steps with Callie nestled in her arms.

"Look who's here, Callie," she cooed. "It's your mommy. She's home."

Mom tilted Callie forward just enough for me to see her precious face. She was sound asleep, her delicate eyelashes fluttering ever-so-slightly, no doubt as she dreamed.

If ever there was a moment I thought my heart would burst from pure joy, this was it. Just seeing them all here—Mom, Dad, Dev, the boys, Callie—a gentle breeze blowing through my hair, the warmth of the sun on my face, and the faint scent of lilacs in the air, I knew. I was home.

You can do this, Marcy, I thought as Dev peeled the boys off my legs.

"Come on, boys, let's let Mommy go inside," he said, turning them both toward the house. They took off like shots, disappearing through the front door, Mom and Dad close behind.

"Ready?" Dev asked.

"More than you know," I said, taking his arm. He gingerly led me up the steps and onto the porch. I took a deep breath, smiled, and nodded at him to let him know I was ready to go inside.

As we stepped into the hallway, I quickly took in as many details as I could, in part hoping something might trigger a memory, and if not, hoping to commit the layout to memory, so I wouldn't get caught stumbling around blindly. As supportive as Mom and Dev had been of my coming home, I sensed that they were still concerned, and I didn't want to give them any reason to think I wasn't ready or that I would benefit from a few days at the rehab center. Now that I was finally here, I was going to stay—no matter what.

I paused in the doorway and looked off to the left at what appeared to be the living room. There was a beautiful fireplace and a gorgeous red couch. The walls were covered in a deep, rich, country-French-blue wallpaper. None of it looked familiar, but one thing was for sure . . . whoever decorated this room had a real flair for color and design.

"Well?" Dev said expectantly, his eyebrows raised in anticipation.

"I'd forgotten how beautiful this room was." *There*, I thought. *That wasn't entirely untrue.*

Dev leaned in and kissed my forehead, breathing a clear sigh of relief. Fortunately, the sound of the boys squealing in the next room drowned out the guilt that was beginning to rise up inside me.

"Boys!" my Mom half shouted, ducking down the hall, still cradling Callie in her arms. "Keep your voices down. You don't want to wake your sister."

Those boys are going to be a handful, I thought, taking a deep, centering breath. Whether it was the aftereffects of the medication or just the natural exhaustion that comes from suffering major medical trauma, I had no idea, but my energy level definitely wasn't where it needed to be to keep up with two rambunctious boys and a newborn. Thank goodness Mom was going to be staying for a few more weeks. There was no question, I was going to need some help.

"Shall we?" Dev said, holding out his hand, a smile on his face as wide as the Mississippi. I smiled back, took his hand, and let him lead me down the hall into the kitchen, where Mom, having settled Callie in a carrier on the counter, was rooting through the refrigerator, undoubtedly looking for a snack for the boys.

The kitchen was striking, with deep, rich, red wallpaper, off-white cabinets, and a series of wonderful old blue and white decorative china plates lining the walls. The countertops were covered in cards, flower arrangements, and empty casserole dishes with sticky notes still stuck to the tops. Dev hadn't been kidding. Our friends really had gone all out. I glanced at the gift tag sticking out of one of the floral arrangements and, not surprisingly, didn't recognize the name. I only hoped I'd be able to learn them all again quickly.

A calendar scribbled with notes hung on the refrigerator next to photos of Conner and Casen and a shot of Callie taken shortly after she was born. Action figures and toy cars were strewn across the linoleum floor. Everywhere I looked were signs of chaos—happy chaos, but chaos nonetheless.

Taking in all the details of my new life, I felt light-headed and put my hand on the countertop for balance.

"Maybe you should go lie down and get some rest, Marcy," Mom suggested. "It's okay. I've got everything under control here." She set plates with freshly cut peanut butter and jelly sandwiches down in front of the boys.

"Actually, that's probably not a bad idea," Dev conceded. "This is the most up and around you've been in weeks. You don't want to overdo it."

As much as I wanted to push back and assure them both that I was fine, the sight of Conner's already sticky, jam-covered face and fingers made me realize I wasn't quite as ready to jump back into full-time motherhood as I thought. *How in the world am I going to manage all of this after Mom's gone?*

"Actually, I *have* been looking forward to sleeping in my own bed." I smiled weakly. Again, not entirely untrue.

Mom set a jam-covered dishrag down on the counter. "Would you like me to help you get settled?"

I was hoping she would say that. I loved the way Mom always took care of me when I was sick.

"That would be great, Mom, thanks."

Mom handed a fresh dish towel to Dev, who went to work mopping up Conner's face, then she wrapped her arm around my waist and slowly guided me back down the hallway to a room opposite the living room. As we turned the corner and peered inside, relief washed over me at the sight of a fluffy, inviting bed.

I paused for a split second. There was something vaguely familiar about this room. I quickly scanned the room—the coral walls, the matching blue and coral linens on the bed, peeking out from beneath a billowy white comforter, and the blue fabric-covered chair in the corner. There was a faint scent of something floral. Perfume perhaps, or maybe just one of the many get-well or welcome home bouquets in the next room. Still . . . there was something . . . What was it? Something about the bed? The smell? The decor?

"Marcy, are you okay?" Mom asked, a concerned expression on her face.

"Oh, I'm fine," I chirped. "I just . . ." *Choose your words carefully.* ". . . really missed this room."

"Well," Mom said, rubbing my back, "you're home now. Come on, let's get you into bed." Mom led me to the bedside and pulled back the sheets. I slipped off my shoes, climbed in, and lay my head back on the cool pillow. Every muscle in my body was sore, but it felt so good to be in a bed with real linens; a soft, cushy pillow; and no tubes, IV bags, or machines beeping incessantly in the background. Mom pulled the comforter up, tucked it under my chin, and the bedding swallowed me up in a cozy, drowsy calm.

"You just get some rest, Marcy," Mom cooed. "Don't worry about the kids. I'm here, there is a nurse coming next week to help with Callie, and of course Tinie will be here to help out too. You're not going to be alone in all this."

"Tinie?" I asked, then quickly bit my tongue. *Be careful.*

"Christine, darling," Mom said, her brow knitting in concern. "Your housekeeper."

"Oh, that's right," I hedged. "Christine. Of course. I—" *Careful* . . . "—the nickname just threw me for a second. I'm still feeling a little woozy from all the meds. I'll be fine after I get a little rest," I assured Mom.

"Of course you will, sweetie." She smiled. "You just get some sleep." She stood up, went over to the window, and closed the shutters, blanketing the room in cool shadows. When she got to the door, she turned and in the gentlest of whispers said, "Welcome home, darling."

Home, I thought, breathing in that faint floral scent that still teased my memory. I settled in beneath the covers, beneath the sheets I didn't remember but had probably picked out myself. *Home*, I thought again before drifting off to sleep.

CHAPTER 10

A PROVIDENTIAL NEIGHBOR

"Are you sure you can't stay a little longer?" I asked as my dad packed away the last of his button-down shirts and zipped up his carry-on bag.

"Sorry, sweetheart, I gotta get back to fillin' teeth. Besides, your mother's here. She's got a good handle on those boys."

"Still . . . I wish you could stay." I felt seventeen all over again.

"Ohhh . . . come here," he said, pulling me into a hug. "You're gonna be just fine, Marcy. Just take it slow. Your mom, Dev, and Tinie are all here to help you."

I knew he was right. Even with Dev back at work, between Mom and Tinie, I'd barely had to lift a finger. Tinie kept the entire house spotless, took care of the laundry, the shopping, and shuttled the boys to and from the park, McDonald's, and playdates with their little friends, and Mom ran the kitchen and hovered over Callie 24-7. Every time I tried to help, I was told to "sit down and relax" or to "go take a nap." Dad was the only one who didn't treat me like an invalid.

"And if you need me," he continued, "I am just a phone call away."

I buried my face in his shoulder. That was just it . . . I couldn't remember his number.

"Jimmy," Mom poked her head in the door. "Your cab's here."

"I'm sorry Dev isn't here to drive you to the airport," I said, wiping my cheeks. Dev had gone back to work two days ago. It had been several weeks since Callie was born, and Dev had been right by my side almost the entire time—but work was piling up.

"Don't worry about me," Dad assured me, pulling his carry-on over his shoulder. "I'm a big boy."

"Boys!" I called out. "Come say goodbye to Doc!" Casen and Conner both scrambled into the room and latched onto Dad's legs. Those boys loved him. He would play in the backyard with them for hours. Where he found the energy, I had no idea. Goodness knows I didn't have it yet.

"Bye, Doc!" Casen beamed up at him. Dad reached down and tousled Casen's hair and then tapped Conner on the head.

"Now you boys mind your mother, okay? Don't make me come back here," he faked a scowl, sending both boys into peals of laughter. Gosh, they adored that man.

"All right, enough now," Mom said, shooing the boys away and seeing Dad to the door.

I gave him one last hug then stood back in the entryway and watched him climb into the cab. Dad had always been such a calming presence. With him nearby, I always felt safe. Confident. Secure. I needed that now more than ever.

As the cab pulled away, he waved and mouthed "I love you" through the window.

If I hadn't known better, I'd have sworn I saw his lower lip quiver.

⌐

"Good morning, sweetie," I cooed, scooping Callie up out of her crib. Getting to spend a little one-on-one time with Callie after the bus picked Casen up for kindergarten and the car pool had taken Conner to preschool had quickly become one of my favorite parts of the day. A quick pat of the hand told me she was due for a change.

It was so strange. Even after weeks at home, there were still things that seemed so foreign to me. I was still finding things in random places, spending too much time looking for things, and I had accidentally wandered into a hall closet thinking it was the den. No matter how long I stared at the family pictures scattered about on the shelves and tabletops, I was able to recognize Dev, the boys, my parents, my sister Ann and my brother Jamey, but I could not, for the life of me, remember a single one of the events or vacations the pictures came from, and I didn't recognize—or particularly like—any of the clothes hanging in my closet. They all seemed . . . older, and much more preppy and conservative than anything I would want to wear. And yet everything about taking care of Callie felt like second nature. From changing diapers to rocking her to sleep, it was all automatic.

Granted, Mom had drawn the short straw most nights, letting me sleep while she sat up with Callie, who was extremely fussy due to the chronic ear infections Dr. Bryan had warned us about. In fact, I rarely even heard her. We had made up the daybed in the nursery for Mom to sleep in, so she typically went to settle Callie down as soon as she started crying. And thank goodness. While God had yet to restore my memory, he *had* gifted me with a full complement of maternal instincts, one of which was the death by a thousand cuts every mother endures when her child cries out in pain.

I already felt bad enough about not being there for Callie during the first two weeks of her life. I couldn't bear the thought of her suffering any further.

"Marcy, honey, do you need any help?" Mom poked her head in the door.

"It's okay, Mom, I've got it. I'm just going to give Callie her medicine."

"Okay, call me if you need anything. I'm going to straighten up a little bit in the kitchen."

I shuddered to think of what it was going to be like when Mom went back to Texas in a couple of weeks. Even with a full night's sleep and a nap during the day while the boys were at school, I was still exhausted all the time.

"I'm okay now, though, aren't I?" I smiled at Callie. She stretched and flexed her little fingers.

I reached over and grabbed the syringe Dr. Bryan had given me to administer Callie's antibiotics. Because of her soft cleft palate, I had to carefully squirt the thick, gooey medication into her mouth.

"Okay, sweetie," I said, propping her head up slightly so the antibiotics would go down easier, "here we go."

I waited for her to settle and then pushed down on the plunger. No sooner did the liquid start to dispense than Callie suddenly inhaled the thick medication. I heard a quick gasping sound, then she started coughing and sputtering, the medicine going everywhere. Then suddenly, she was struggling to catch her breath.

"Mom!" I screamed in a panic. "Mom! Callie's struggling to breathe!"

Mom raced into the room, her eyes wide as saucers. "What happened?"

"She took a breath just as I was pushing the plunger down, and now she . . . she can't catch her breath!" I was nearly hysterical.

"Call the paramedics!" Mom said, taking Callie from me.

I raced into my bedroom and grabbed the receiver off the phone next to my bed. My hands were shaking uncontrollably. I stared at the keypad and froze. *What's the number?* "Mom, what's the number?" I shouted.

"Marcy?" Mom rushed into the room, a choking Callie in her arms.

"I can't remember the number!" I wailed, hot tears flowing down my cheeks.

"9-1-1," Mom said, her own voice tinged with panic.

I quickly punched it in.

A female voice came on the line. "9-1-1, what is your emergency?"

"Yes, I need help!" I all but shouted. "My baby isn't breathing! I think she's choking!"

"I understand. What is your address, ma'am?"

I had no idea. *Oh, God!*

"Mom, Mom! What's our address?" I stammered.

"Give me the phone," she said, snatching the receiver from my hand. "Hello? Yes, we're at . . ." I just stood by in horror as my mom rattled off the address of the home I'd lived in for over a year but could not have located on a map if my life depended on it. But my life didn't depend on it. *Callie's* did.

Oh, please, Lord, don't let anything happen to Callie. Please let her be okay.

"What? You've got to be kidding me! What are we supposed to do?" Mom looked as though she had just seen a ghost.

"What?" I searched her face frantically for clues. "What's happening?"

"Well, please, hurry!" she said, her eyes filling with tears.

"Mom, what's happening?"

She hung up the phone and shook her head. "Randolph Road and Providence Road are both backed up because of accidents. The paramedics may have a hard time getting to us."

I felt all the air leave my lungs, and it was all I could do not to collapse onto the floor. I looked down at Callie, still unresponsive in Mom's arms. A high-pitched humming sound filled my ears. "What are we supposed to do?"

Mom just stared at me, helpless. "I . . ."

Just then, there was a banging at the front door, and the door opened. A man I had never seen before rushed in, spotting us in the bedroom. He was wearing khaki shorts and a gray T-shirt. He was sweaty and smelled of freshly cut grass.

"Paramedic," he said, taking Callie from my mom. He laid Callie down on the sofa in the living room and immediately started working to clear her airway. Mom and I just stood back and looked on in horror. Mom was crying, and I could not stop shaking. After several seconds that felt like hours, Callie sputtered, coughed, and then let loose the most beautiful wail I had ever heard. My knees went out from under me, and I dropped to the floor in tears.

Thank you, Lord, Oh thank you!

"Oh . . . thank you so much . . ." My mom stared blankly at the young man.

"Keith." He nodded at her. "I live four houses down. I was mowing the lawn, I went inside to get a drink of water and heard the call come in over the scanner. As soon as I heard the address, I started running."

Dear God.

"Oh, thank you!" my mom gushed, the tears flowing freely.

"You're welcome," he said, continuing to give Callie a rudimentary exam. "I've cleared her airway, and she seems to be breathing okay, but it's labored. As soon as the ambulance gets here, you'll want to take her to the hospital to get checked out. How old is she?"

"Five weeks," I said. I reached out and stroked her head. She was so tiny. So helpless. And she knew about as much about the world she'd been born into as I did.

While Keith continued to work with Callie, I called Dev, told him what happened, and asked him to come home right away. Several minutes later, the humming in my ears was replaced by the welcome sound of a siren in the distance. Soon, two more paramedics joined us in the kitchen, followed almost immediately by an out-of-breath Dev.

There was a lot of commotion as the paramedics continued to evaluate Callie, then one of them turned to me and said, "She's stable. We're going to go take her to the hospital."

Without even thinking, I blurted out, "I'm coming with you."

"I'm sorry, ma'am, you can't ride in the ambulance with her, but you can follow behind us."

He had to be kidding me. I opened my mouth to protest, but Dev quickly stepped in.

"Thank you, we'll do that," he said, gripping both of my arms tight to keep me from following them.

"Mom, you're coming with us?" I half asked, half commanded.

"I better stay here, sweetie," she said, checking her watch. "It's almost lunchtime. The boys will be coming home from school soon."

The boys. I had totally forgotten.

"You two go," she said, shooing us toward the door. "Go be with Callie."

I wrapped Mom in a hug. "Thank you, Mom. I don't know what I would have done . . ."

"I know, sweetie," she said, patting my back. "It's okay. She's okay."

I looked at Mom, and a fresh set of tears welled up in my eyes. How close had I just come to losing Callie? I couldn't remember the phone number. I couldn't remember our address. If she hadn't been there . . .

"Marcy . . ." Dev said, his keys in his hand. "Let's go."

"Go," Mom said. I could tell by her expression she knew exactly what I was thinking.

I nodded at Dev and wiped my nose on my sleeve. "We'll call as soon as we get there," I promised her. "Kiss the boys for me. Don't let them worry."

I followed Dev out to his car and collapsed into the front seat. He backed out of the driveway and idled in the street for a moment, waiting for the ambulance to pull away. I stared at the back of the vehicle, my stomach churning at the thought of my precious little girl inside, sick, frightened, and surrounded by strangers. What a horrific experience.

As the ambulance pulled away, I looked back at the house and saw Keith standing on the front lawn, shielding his eyes from the sun watching us, and I wept.

Thank you, God. Thank you so much.

⌒

As soon as we came within sight of the hospital, my heart began to race. My hands felt clammy, and my head felt hot.

"I'm going to park out by Emergency," Dev said. "Do you want me to drop you off by the door?"

"No." I couldn't bear the thought of walking back through those doors by myself. "We'll go in together."

Dev found a spot and quickly raced around the front of the car to help me get out. "Take it easy, babe. You've had a rough morning."

"I'm fine, Dev," I lied. "Let's just go see Callie."

When we walked through the automatic doors and the first whiff of antiseptic hit my nostrils, I thought I might pass out. I had worked so hard to get out of here, and now, just a few weeks later, here I was again. My heart was practically pounding out of my chest.

Dev checked us in at the desk, and I hung back slightly, hoping against all hope nobody on the staff would recognize the woman they didn't think was ready to go home. Whose infant daughter had just been brought in by ambulance.

The next few hours were interminable. Callie had an entire team of people working on her, and they ran every test known to man— X-rays, EKGs, ultrasounds, urinalysis, blood work—the whole nine yards.

Finally, around four o'clock, Dr. Bryan, whom Dev had called after we arrived, came out to see us.

"How is she, Blair?" Dev asked, too upset to bother with formalities. "Is she okay?"

He sat down across from us in the waiting area. "The good news is, all of the tests have come back negative. Some of her blood counts are a bit off, but given the infection, that's to be expected."

"But . . ." Dev asked, gripping my hand.

"For some reason, she isn't responding. She's extremely lethargic, and she's struggling to clear her own airway."

"What does that mean?" I asked.

"The technical term is 'failure to thrive,'" he said. "We think it may have something to do with the fact that she was separated from you for so long, so early," he said, looking at me, and my heart sank.

This is my fault. I wasn't there for her when she needed me, and now . . .

Dev squeezed my hand. "Is there anything we can do?"

"There is," he said. "We're going to have to keep Callie here for a few days for observation in a special isolation room that will protect her from picking up any further infections."

"Isolation," Dev broke in, "but you just said . . ."

"I know," Dr. Bryan said. "But what I am suggesting is that you stay here with her, Marcy. What Callie needs right now more than anything is time with you. Time to bond." He held my eye. "Right now, you're the best medicine she can get. She needs you."

"Of course, I'll stay with her," I said. "Can I see her now?"

Dr. Bryan nodded and stood up. "They're just bringing her upstairs now. We'll get a bed set up for you, and then yes, you can see her. Dev," he continued, "I'm afraid you won't be able to stay the night. It's important that we limit outside contact with Callie as much as possible to reduce the chance of infection. For now, anyway, Marcy will be the only one who can stay."

Dev looked crushed, but to his credit, not wanting to upset me further, he quickly recovered. "You okay?" he asked, his eyes showing more than a hint of concern.

Honestly, I wasn't. Just being in this building felt oppressive. Everything about it was abhorrent to me—the smell, the incessant beeping, the cold, sterile, colorless concrete walls—but Callie needed me. And from the moment we walked through those doors, I knew there was no way I was leaving without her.

I nodded. "I'll be fine. You go home. Take care of the boys. See if Tinie can come by an extra day or two to help Mom out."

After Dev and I said our goodbyes, Dr. Bryan brought me upstairs to the isolation room. Callie was lying in a crib, fast asleep, and just to the right of it was a hospital bed. With shiny metal rails. And crumpled white sheets. My hands felt clammy again and my heart began to race. I took a deep breath and tried to center myself. It wasn't working.

I walked over to the crib and carefully picked up Callie. She looked so tiny. I could have worn her little wristband on two of my fingers. I gently stroked her cheek and kissed the top of her head.

"It's okay, sweetie. Mommy's here," I whispered. "And she's never going to leave you again. Ever."

There was a nursing chair in the corner, so I went over and sat down to rock Callie for a while. She was the only sign of life in an otherwise sterile, lifeless room. I hated that we were here. But at least we were here together. I cradled her close to my chest, and as we rocked, my heart slowed to a gentle rhythmic beat. Callie yawned, her eyes opened briefly, and she looked up at me. I smiled, leaned down, and kissed her little nose.

"You're going to be okay," I promised her. "We're both going to be okay."

———

For the next several days, all I did was hold Callie and love on her. She mostly slept, but by the end of the third day, her numbers were starting to even out. Dr. Bryan had been right. All Callie needed was me.

Dev called several times a day to check on us. It was torture not seeing the boys, and Mom said that Conner was taking the separation particularly hard. He was afraid I wasn't going to come home again—like last time. Dad even came for a few days, which helped immensely. The boys loved Dad, so having him there was a perfect distraction for Conner. It was also a tremendous help to me.

The week after Callie was released, the doctors put tubes in her ears to help keep the infections from getting out of control until she was strong enough to undergo surgery to correct her soft cleft palate. Normally, they would put her under for that procedure, but given Callie's fragile condition, the doctor needed to do it while she was fully awake. Enter Dad.

"Don't worry, sweetheart," he said as I stood quaking in the waiting room, "I've got this." And with that, he followed the doctor into the exam room and held Callie still while they inserted the tubes. It was awful. I could hear her screaming halfway down the hall. And yet, just knowing that my dad was in there with her set my heart and mind at ease.

As word got out to friends and neighbors, a fresh batch of casseroles arrived at our doorstep, and the parents of Casen and Conner's little friends arranged daily playdates to keep the boys busy and give me more one-on-one time with Callie. I had dreaded the daily interactions with people I was certain not to remember, but Dev kept most of them at bay, using the excuse of needing to keep the house quiet for Callie. Either he or Mom answered the phone and the door, keeping everyone up-to-date on Callie's progress and passing along everyone's well-wishes and prayers.

Dad left the day after Callie had her tubes put in, but Mom stayed with us for another week. Dev volunteered to drive her to the airport, but Mom insisted she take a cab. She tried to pass it off as a favor to Dev, who had already missed far too much time at work, but I suspected she was just nervous about leaving me alone at the house with

Callie. To her credit, she never told Dev about the 9-1-1 mishap, and for that, I was grateful. I was still struggling to find my way around the house, and if Tinie hadn't taken control of car pools and handled all the cleaning and picking up, I think more eyebrows would have been raised about my ability to handle things around the house.

The morning Mom left, I stood in the doorway holding Callie, my best "Don't worry—I've got this" face on, but inside I was terrified. Nothing had gone as smoothly as I had hoped. In fact, my first several weeks home had been disastrous. Dev practically had to pry Conner off of my leg every morning to get him to preschool because he was afraid I wasn't going to be there when he got back. It was at once flattering and incredibly defeating. Even when I was here, I couldn't seem to be what these kids needed.

And now, a month and a half after waking up from the coma . . . I still couldn't remember anything about the last thirteen years.

CHAPTER 11

OFF COURSE

"Can I drive?" I asked Dev one day as we headed toward the car. He paused and raised his eyebrows, no doubt wondering the same thing I was. *Could I?*

"Are you sure?" he asked, hesitantly holding out the keys. I had been home about three weeks at that point, so he was somewhat justified in being skeptical—but I took the keys from his hand nonetheless. Dev thought it would be a good idea for us to drive around the neighborhood so I could reorient myself, so while the boys were both at a playdate and Tinie was there to keep an eye on Callie, we decided to give it a go. I understood Dev's hesitation, but I needed to start driving again. With Mom leaving soon and Tinie only coming in two days a week, that left me on my own quite a bit, and Callie would need to go to the doctor for her wellness checkups.

"I'm going to have to drive Callie to the doctor," I reminded him. "And those casseroles aren't going to last forever. Eventually,

I'm going to have to go to the store." As soon as I said it, I realized I wasn't even sure where the store was. But one hurdle at a time.

"Okay . . ." he said, dropping the keys into my hand, "here you go."

I sat down behind the wheel of our Volvo station wagon, turned the key in the ignition, put the car in reverse, and slowly backed out of the driveway. When I glanced over, I noticed Dev had one hand on the dashboard and the other on the ceiling, as though he was bracing for a crash.

"Relax, Dev . . ." I laughed. "I've got it." And oddly enough . . . I did. I had no idea where I was going, but the act of actually driving felt like second nature. Dev guided me around the neighborhood, pointing out houses where friends of ours lived. The morning was going so smoothly, I didn't dare let on that none of the names he was rattling off rang a bell. He also showed me how to get to the grocery store, Conner's preschool, and Callie's doctor's office. "What's the quickest way there?" I had asked, hoping he wouldn't catch on. Meanwhile, I tried to keep a running tab in my head of all the street names, many of which seemed to be called Sharon, for some reason.

I reached down and turned on the radio. James Taylor's "How Sweet It Is" filled the car, and before I knew it, I was singing along.

"I can't believe you remember the words to this." Dev laughed. "I haven't heard this song in years."

Now that he mentioned it . . . neither had I. A smile swept across my face. I could drive. I almost had some idea where I was going. And I remembered the lyrics to a song I hadn't heard since college.

Maybe I was going to be all right after all.

A few weeks later, after Callie's tubes were put in, the boys and I were just finishing up our afternoon snack when the doorbell rang.

Who could that be?

I walked to the front door. I glanced out the window and saw a young woman standing on the porch. She didn't look familiar.

I opened the door hesitantly.

"Hi, Marcy!" She beamed. "It's so good to finally see you!"

"It's good to see you, too." I smiled back.

"How are you feeling? I heard about poor Callie."

"We're both doing fine, thanks. It's so sweet of you to stop by."

She hoisted up a large casserole dish in a quilted carrier, with an even larger covered bowl resting on top. "The other women at church and I wanted to pitch in with meals, so I signed up to bring over some dinner. Just some chicken tetrazzini, a salad, and some rolls."

"Oh, that's so kind of you," I said, taking the stack of items from her. "Thank you!"

The woman stood awkwardly for a few moments, looking past me into the front hall. I knew I should ask her in—but I wasn't sure how much longer I could carry on small talk with a complete stranger without giving myself away. Instead, I just stood still in the doorway and smiled, hoping she would take the hint.

"Well, please tell everyone at church I said hello and that we're doing well," I said, taking a slight step back.

"Will do, Marcy. We're all praying for you and the kids."

That was so sweet. "Thank you," I said sincerely. "I really appreciate that. We all do."

"Will you and Dev be in church on Sunday?" she asked. "I'm just dying to see little Callie."

I thought about that for a second. I did want to go to church. It had been . . . actually, I had no idea how long it had been since I was there last. But the thought of being accosted by dozens of well-meaning strangers asking me questions about Dev and the kids, some of which I might be able to fake my way through, but many of which I wouldn't, made my stomach hurt.

"Possibly," I said. "We're still keeping a close eye on Callie, so . . ."

"I understand," she said sympathetically. "Well . . . you take care of yourself. And call me if you need anything, okay?"

"I will. Thank you." I stepped back, closed the door, and breathed a sigh of relief.

"Who was at the door, Mommy?" Casen asked.

I have no idea. "One of Mommy and Daddy's friends from church." I smiled down at him. "Look. She brought us some chicken for dinner tonight."

"More chicken?" he said, scrunching up his face.

He was right. Eventually, I was going to have to venture into the kitchen to make something non-casserole related.

"I'm sure it's delicious," I said. "Now you go play with your brother, and don't make too much noise. Your sister is still sleeping." Casen dashed off, and I set the carrier on the kitchen counter. I quickly scanned the containers for some kind of tag or note that might provide some hint of who was just here.

Nothing.

I glanced at the ever-growing pile of empty Tupperware and Pyrex dishes on the far end of the counter that would eventually have to be returned and wondered how in the world I would ever figure out what went to whom. I was just about to go check on the boys when I smelled something burning.

I glanced at the plates the boys had left. We'd had grapes and strawberries as a snack. *Fruit doesn't burn.* Sniffing, I turned around to see a pot angrily boiling over onto the stovetop. *Oh, shoot! Not again.* I quickly turned off the burner, removed the pot from the flame, and grabbed a pair of tongs from the drawer. As I pulled the rubber nipples for Callie's bottles out of the scalding water, I could see they were splotched with dark brown spots.

Shoot. That's the third set this week.

I sighed as I gathered them into a paper towel and tossed them into the trash. That was something else I didn't dare tell Dev. Not only had my long-term memories not come back, I was also having problems with short-term ones as well—forgetting Callie's nipples on the stove, blanking on where we kept the laundry detergent, forgetting to go out and meet Casen at the bus stop at the end of the day. And who knows how many times I had gotten up and wandered into the kitchen only to forget what I was going in there for.

I opened the refrigerator to put the salad in until dinner and noticed that aside from a half gallon of milk, a few unidentifiable leftovers from previous casseroles, and a random assortment of condiments, all we really had left to eat was the chicken tetrazzini that had just been dropped off.

"Boys!" I called out. "Put your shoes on."

"Why?" Casen came around the corner, Conner trailing two steps behind. "Where are we going?"

"We," I announced, "are going to the grocery store. And . . ." I bent down to look them both in the eye, "if you're on your best behavior, maybe we can even pick out some ice cream for dessert."

"Yes!" Casen pumped his fist. "I want mint chocolate chip!"

"No." Conner pushed in front of him. "Chocolate!"

"Well . . . if you're really good, maybe we'll get both. Now go get those shoes on!"

The boys both raced back to their bedroom, and I quietly opened the door to Callie's nursery. She was sound asleep. I hated to wake her, but now that the boys had ice cream on the brain, there was no way I was going to be able to stall them. I quietly tiptoed over and gently lifted her out of her crib. Her delicate hands curled into tiny fists as she yawned and peered up at me, and my heart melted.

"I swear, little one, these moments with you and the boys are what keep me going," I cooed, kissing her forehead.

Once everyone was all shoed-up and buckled in, we pulled out of the driveway and headed to the Harris Teeter grocery store about a mile from home. I had learned the way with Dev and now traveled the memorized route frequently.

After wrangling Callie into a carrier attached to the grocery cart, Casen and Conner hung on to either side of the basket, and we made our way to the produce section. I had decided to make a meatloaf. Mom had left me a recipe, and it seemed simple enough. Ground beef, veggies, breadcrumbs, a few assorted herbs and spices. Surely even I could manage that. Besides, it was one of the few dishes nobody had brought us, so it would be a welcome change for the boys, who, according to Casen, were thoroughly chickened out.

We slowly but surely made our way up and down every aisle. I had been there several times, but I still struggled to remember where all the different ingredients might be. For their part, the boys kept it together pretty well. Nothing like the promise of ice cream to keep two otherwise rambunctious boys in line. By the time we made it to the checkout line, however, the boys were picking at each other and Callie was starting to fuss. Any confidence I might have felt coming in quickly gave way to fatigue as I set one item after another, some of which I didn't even remember picking up, on the checkout counter.

As the clerk rang up the last few items, I opened my purse, looked at my checkbook, thought better of it, and instead grabbed my wallet and handed her a wad of bills, hoping it would be enough. The cashier counted them out while I kept my eyes on Casen and Conner, who were fiddling with candy bars in the checkout aisle.

"Here you go." She smiled at me, handing me two singles and some change.

Wow, that was lucky. I took the receipt and stuffed it in my purse. I didn't even want to know how much we'd just spent.

"Would you like some help out to your car?" the boy bagging our groceries asked.

"Oh, that would be wonderful, thank you." I turned to Conner and Casen. "Come on, boys, let's go."

"Can we get a candy bar?" Casen asked, holding up a Snickers bar.

"No, sweetie, we've got ice cream, remember?"

He set the candy bar back down with a pout. Apparently the ice cream wasn't quite the pot of gold it was when we got here.

Our cart brimming with bags, I took Callie out of her little carrier and let the bagger push the cart to the lot.

"Where's your car, ma'am?" he asked.

I scanned the lot. I had no idea. I couldn't even remember what it looked like. I looked down to find Casen with Conner in a wrestling hold and Callie starting to whimper. I glanced back at the bagger, who stared at me with his eyebrows raised, and my heart started to race.

"Casen, honey? Do you remember where Mommy parked the car?"

He let go of Conner, stood up on his tiptoes and pointed. "There."

Well that took care of two birds with one stone.

"That's right. Thank you, sweetie." I smiled at the bagger. "They all look so much alike, don't they?"

"Yes, ma'am," he agreed politely.

While the young man loaded all of our bags into the back, I buckled Callie and Conner into their car seats. "Mom, I have to go to the bathroom!" Casen called out.

"Just hold tight, honey, we'll be home in a few minutes," I assured him, hopping into the driver's seat. It was just after four o'clock. We had been in the store for over an hour. No wonder the kids were getting fussy.

I turned out of the parking lot onto Sharon Amity, a busy four-lane road. I sped through a traffic signal with a large church on the left and one on the right.

. . . Another traffic light, Arbor Way. But we didn't take Arbor Way to get to the store . . .

I glanced in the rearview mirror to see Callie squirming in her car seat and Conner playing with the lock.

"Conner, honey, please don't play with that."

Wait, now I'm on Sharon Lane, not Sharon Amity? When did that happen?

"Mom, I have to go!"

"Casen, I said we'll be home soon."

Callie started to whimper.

"Mom!" Casen repeated.

"I know, sweetie. We're almost there."

The road came to a fork.

Do I go right or left? Nothing looked familiar. I must have missed my turn somehow. I chose right for no other reason than I was in that lane. Then I noticed the street sign for the road I was turning onto.

Sharon Road. What in the world? Why are so many streets in this city called Sharon?

I made the turn and continued to drive, winding through streets lined with beautiful houses. But soon Callie's whimpering turned into a full-on cry.

"I know, baby girl, it's okay," I said, trying to reach back between the seats and touch her foot.

"Mom!" Conner called out. "I have to go, too!"

Great.

I looked down at the clock. We had been driving for more than twenty minutes. *That can't be. The store is less than a mile from our house. Where are we? Lord, please help me. I have no idea where I am or how to get home.*

I turned to the right. Finally, a street that I recognized! I let out a sigh of relief as our house slowly came into view.

"Okay, we're home, boys!" I said as we pulled into our driveway, trying to stay chipper even though every one of my nerves was fried. "That was an adventure, wasn't it?"

Casen tore out of the car and raced to the front door, where he stood dancing on one foot. I quickly let him in then came back to the car to unbuckle Conner and a now-screaming Callie.

Conner made a beeline to the front door, leaving me behind to contend with Callie and a car full of groceries. It took me forever to unload the car, carrying Callie in one arm and one bag at a time in the other. The fact that it was a sweltering 83 degrees wasn't helping.

I had just carried the last bag up to the porch when I felt it shift in my arm. Then I heard a loud splat and my leg suddenly felt cold and wet. I looked down. The bottom of the bag had completely soaked through, and Casen's now half-melted mint chocolate chip ice cream had fallen to the ground and splattered all over the steps.

I could have cried.

So much for a simple trip to the store.

CHAPTER 12

TURNING UP THE HEAT

A hunk of ground beef lying in a bowl stared up at me from the counter.

I glanced at the recipe Mom had left me.

It's a meatloaf, Marcy. How hard can it be?

Two tablespoons of cumin. I remembered buying that the other day; the question was, where had I put it?

I opened and closed a few cabinets, coming across hordes of cooking gadgets I didn't recognize, much less see myself using. I finally stumbled across the lazy Susan filled with little spice jars in the cabinet next to the refrigerator. I pulled out the cumin and some chili powder and sprinkled both on the meat before adding a dollop of ketchup and mustard, mashing everything together by hand, and forming a loaf on a baking sheet.

There, that was easy enough.

I shot a quick glance over my shoulder into the den where the boys were watching cartoons.

I looked at the recipe. Bake at 350 for one hour.

I slid the sheet onto the center rack of the oven and then stared at the knobs.

Which one is the temperature, and which one is the timer?

I fiddled with one of the knobs until the display read 350, then I glanced at the clock. It was four thirty—Dev would be home soon. I turned the temperature a little higher.

The meatloaf well in hand, I turned my attention to the side dishes—green beans and mashed potatoes. A brief scavenger hunt through the cabinets under the counter revealed a large pot. I cut up the potatoes and dropped them into the pot to boil, careful not to turn the heat up too high, lest they meet the same tragic end as the bottle nipples. Then I fanned the green beans out in a pan, sliced in a few squares of butter, added a dollop of minced garlic, and set them on low.

Well . . . that wasn't so hard.

As I stirred the green beans and kept my eye on the potatoes, I heard the front door click open. Casen and Conner took off for the doorway like a starter pistol had just been fired.

"Daddy!"

"Hey, boys!" Dev bent down and scooped Conner up.

"Dev, you're home early!" I said, leaving the green beans to sauté.

"Yeah . . . I thought I'd surprise the boys," he said, then sniffed the air. "Is that garlic?"

"Mmmm hmmm." I smiled. "I was planning a little surprise myself. I'm making meatloaf, mashed potatoes, and green beans for dinner tonight. I figured it was time I finally made a proper meal."

"Oh, you didn't have to do that," he said.

"No . . . we've done enough eating out of Tupperware and off of paper plates. It's time things got back to normal around here."

"Is there anything I can do to help?" Dev asked.

I shook my head. I was determined to do this on my own. After the grocery store fiasco the other day, I needed to prove to myself that I was capable of handling the house and the kids without Mom's help. If I couldn't even make a simple dinner . . .

"Why don't you and the boys go play in the backyard?" I suggested. "I'll call you when dinner's ready."

"You sure?" Dev arched his eyebrows.

No. "Positive."

"Okay, boys." Dev reached down and herded the boys toward the back door. "What do you say we go outside and play so Mommy can finish dinner?"

I stood at the window and watched them for a few minutes. This was how it was supposed to be. Dev and the boys playing out back, Callie asleep in her nursery, and me making dinner for my family.

I turned back to the project at hand. *Might as well set the table.*

I really hadn't set the table since I got home, what with Mom and Tinie shooing me out of the kitchen every time I tried to help. In my search for flatware I unearthed some lovely cloth napkins. If I was going to do this, I was going to do it right. I went into the dining room and looked at the antique mahogany table. I folded the napkins and set one down next to each place mat, but when I went to set down the first fork, I couldn't remember if it went on the left or the right side of the plate.

Does the fork go next to the knife or the spoon? Or is that the one that's off by itself?

After several minutes of trying different arrangements, nothing looked right. I wasn't even sure I had the napkins in the right spots. *Come on, Marcy, you learned this as a child . . . this is so frustrating. Why can't I picture it? Picture . . .*

I ran back to the kitchen and grabbed a cookbook from the shelf. On the front was a photo of an elegant dinner table set for four.

So forks on the left, then knife and spoon on the right, and glasses in the upper-right corner . . .

As I was adjusting the place settings, I smelled a faint whiff of smoke and heard a familiar hiss from the stove. The beans and potatoes! I raced into the kitchen, where I turned off the burners.

The potatoes looked okay despite boiling over a little. I transferred them into a bowl, added some milk and butter, and got to work mashing them. I looked out the window again at Dev and the boys. Casen caught my eye and waved. *How I loved those kids.*

Casen motioned me to come outside, so I put down the potatoes and stepped into the yard. Dev was coaching Casen in T-ball, and when Casen swung the bat and made solid contact, he looked at me for approval.

I gave him a huge smile. "Way to go!"

When I came back into the house, I noticed thin trails of smoke pouring out of the sides of the oven. *The meatloaf!*

I raced over to the oven and looked at the display. It read 500.

500! How did . . . ? Then I realized—I'd been afraid the meatloaf would take too long, so I'd turned up the heat.

I grabbed the oven mitts and opened the door.

I was almost afraid to look.

What I pulled out was no longer anything resembling food but a black brick covered in sticky char. More smoke wafted upward.

I quickly grabbed a magazine off the counter and tried to fan it away from the alarm before it went off and woke . . .

Callie.

Too late. The screams were almost simultaneous, first the smoke detector, followed immediately by Callie. I rushed into the nursery to find Callie red-faced and wailing.

"I'm sorry, sweetie. I'm so sorry. It's okay. It's okay." I picked her up and pressed her tight against my chest.

"Marcy!" Dev called out from the kitchen. "What's going on?"

I rushed back to the kitchen cradling a still screaming Callie to find Dev standing on a chair, pushing the silencer on the smoke detector.

"Oh, Dev . . ." I started to cry. "I burned the meatloaf." I pointed to the charred brick sitting on top of the stove. "I'm so sorry."

Dev surveyed the damage and then stepped toward me. "Honey, it's fine. We'll just heat up some of the leftovers in the fridge."

"But I'm supposed to know how to do this," I sobbed. "What kind of wife and mother doesn't know how to cook dinner for her family?"

Dev rested his hands on my shoulders and looked me in the eye. "You are a wonderful wife and mother, Marcy. You always have been. That hasn't changed. Maybe you're trying to do too much too soon," he suggested. "Things will get easier. You just need a little more time, that's all."

But it *wasn't* getting easier. And with Mom gone, three kids, a husband, and a house to take care of, I didn't have more time. Not being able to remember the past thirteen years was devastating enough, but not even being able to manage simple chores like driving home from the store or setting the temperature on the oven . . . I felt like such a failure.

"Something smells like burning!" Casen said, bursting through the back door, Conner right behind him.

"Yes, sweetie." I sniffed. "Mommy burned the meatloaf."

"Yesss!" Casen chirped, pumping his fist in the air. "We *hate* meatloaf!"

Well . . . at least there's that.

⟋

The next morning, hazy light streaming from the window cast our bedroom in a glow and woke me from another fitful sleep. I rubbed my eyes and looked over at Dev, sound asleep next to me.

He had to know I was struggling. Last night's dinner of mashed potatoes, green beans, and cold cereal was evidence of that. But he didn't know how badly I was struggling. Neither did anyone else for that matter.

There had been moments over the past few weeks when I had wanted to tell Dev the truth: that my long-term memories weren't coming back and that my short-term memory wasn't strong either. When we were getting ready for bed or watching TV on the couch, I'd look at him and think, *Just tell him, Marcy*. I knew he would respond with compassion. But then, my mind would reel from the possible consequences: rehab, hospital, being away from the kids again. And what if the rehab didn't even help? If the memory issues were the result of swelling around the brain, as the doctors all said, it should have resolved itself weeks ago. What if there was something else wrong? Something that couldn't be fixed? Given the choice, I would rather be alone in my confusion at home than alone in a hospital room away from my family. And if there was something wrong with my brain that couldn't be fixed, I wasn't sure I wanted to know. Better to live with hope than to have it all dashed.

The only person I did confess the truth of my situation to was God. Every morning, after Dev left for work and the boys for school, while Callie was still sleeping, I would sit at the kitchen table and pray. I would confess to the Lord—and myself—that I was not handling the role of wife and mother well. That my brain was not getting better. That the memories were not coming back. That I was in over my head. That I needed help—help I was afraid to ask for.

I would turn to the passage in Lamentations that our pastor, David Chadwick, had prayed over me while I had been in the coma and read it again and again:

Because of the LORD's great love we are not consumed,
    for his compassions never fail.
They are new every morning;
    great is your faithfulness. (NIV)

Easter with my sweet sister, Ann, and my brother, Jamey, who always kept us laughing. Behind us is our dog Susie, wiped out from playing, while our new puppy is hiding in Ann's lap!

Showing my little sister around campus during my freshman year of college, dressed up as part of a singing group. I was seventeen—the age I thought I was when I awoke from the coma thirteen years later. **This is the face I expected to see in the mirror.**

Sorority initiation weekend. I was bursting with joy at being able to share this special experience with my mom and dad.

I remember this party—the first one Dev and I went to as a couple. Already, I knew I was crazy about him.

Our wedding, December 20, 1980. **When I look at this image, my mind is completely blank— it's like looking at a picture of other people.** Years later, I would try on my wedding dress in a desperate attempt to remember this day.

Minutes after Callie was born, March 1990. Days later, when I awoke from my coma, this picture confused me so much.

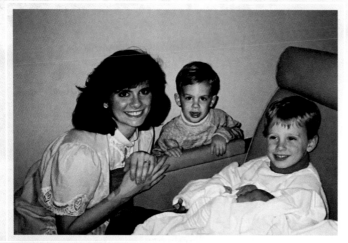

The first time the boys came to see Callie. Soon afterward, I fell into the coma—and when I awoke, I had no memory of these three precious children.

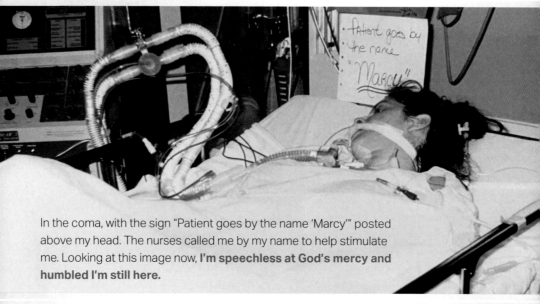

In the coma, with the sign "Patient goes by the name 'Marcy'" posted above my head. The nurses called me by my name to help stimulate me. Looking at this image now, **I'm speechless at God's mercy and humbled I'm still here.**

Me, Jamey, and Ann at the beach, summer 1990. This trip was the first time I relaxed and felt normal after the coma. I still had my memories from childhood, so I didn't have to pretend when I was talking with them.

A family picture for our Christmas card, 1991. Little did everyone know that I was desperately trying to fake being okay—and had started drinking.

RIGHT:
Tinie has a special bond with each of my kids. Here she is with Conner—his foot was hurt, but she came to every football game even if he was on the sidelines.

BELOW:
A big family trip to celebrate Casen's graduation from college and Conner's from high school. I treasured this time with my older kids—mature and ready to launch.

ABOVE:
Working in my first studio.

LEFT:
Gathered with family at my gallery show "Expressions of Joy," in 2015.

BELOW:
Tinie reading my bio and looking at "Lost and Found."

Walking down the aisle at Callie's wedding with my two boys.

My baby girl, all grown up and getting married.

France in 2018 with our "Friends like Family" group. This was the very last time I felt good before the rheumatoid arthritis hit.

Ann, mom, and me.

Adrian and I became dear friends when we started painting in the same studio, and now we can finish each other's sentences!

Taste and see that the Lord is good; blessed is the one who takes refuge in him. Psalm 34:8

I begin my work with a verse— this is the underpainting.

Putting tennis balls on my paintbrushes helps me hold them and gives me a longer amount of time in the studio before the pain in my hands becomes too great.

Our family. I am blessed beyond measure.
Conner and Megan; Joseph, Callie, and baby Grayson;
me and Dev; Wyatt, Casen, Megan, and Hudson

I knew this last line to be true. The Lord had been faithful to me. He saved my life. Even the doctors said it was a miracle that I came out of the coma. There was no other explanation. He also saved Callie. How else could one explain Keith stepping into his kitchen at the exact moment my mom's frantic 9-1-1 call came over the scanner?

And I saw with my own eyes the new gifts God provided every morning: a patient and loving husband who'd never left my side; two precious boys and a beautiful baby girl who loved me unconditionally; caring friends who kept us fed for weeks and prayed for us constantly. Everywhere I looked, I saw daily reminders of God's provision and care . . . even amid the mess.

I smiled as I thought about the nightly routine that the boys and Callie and I had created. I would bring Callie into the boys' room and we'd read stories and sing. Last night, the boys and I sang "Angels Watching over Callie," and Callie flashed us a smile so wide, I almost forgot the entire meatloaf fiasco. Little moments like those made all the struggles seem worthwhile. And God had given me just enough of them to get me through each day.

I quietly slipped out of bed, grabbed my Bible, and made my way to the kitchen. I could still smell a faint whiff of burnt meat in the air. I opened my Bible to Lamentations and skipped down to verse 3:24.

I say to myself, "The Lord is my portion;
therefore I will wait for him." (NIV)

The word *wait* jumped off the page at me and pricked my heart.

Lord, please heal me. I've been waiting for so long, and everything is still so confusing. It's just not getting any better. I should be able to get to and from the grocery store and make a simple meal without issues. But every day I just feel so inadequate . . . and alone. I know I haven't made things any easier on myself by keeping my problems a secret, but I'm afraid that if I do say something, they'll take me away from my children again, and I can't let that happen. Casen seems to be managing okay, but Conner is really struggling, and my confusion almost killed poor Callie. Lord, I don't know what to do.

I turned to another earmarked page of Scripture, Romans 8. I had returned to this passage more times than I could count in recent weeks, but verse 28 still struck right at my soul every time I read it:

And we know that in all things God works for the good of those who love him, who have been called according to his purpose. (NIV)

I put my Bible down and closed my eyes.

Lord, I believe you are working in this situation for my good. But I can't see the good in this right now. I'm such a mess. Please heal me. Please heal my brain. Please restore my lost memories—the memories of marrying Dev and having the kids and raising them. You saved my life, and for that, Lord, I thank you. Thank you. Thank you. But Lord, I've just lost so much. So much that I'm not willing to give up. Please, Lord, help me to remember.

I opened my eyes and glanced around the kitchen that still felt as foreign to me as it did when I first came home two months ago. The silence was deafening.

CHAPTER 13

A BEACH GETAWAY

"Darling, why don't you come down to Texas for a few days." Mom's suggestion washed over me like a cool, soothing breeze on a hot Charlotte afternoon. It had only been two weeks since she had left, but between the grocery store mishap, the meatloaf fiasco, the never-ending trips back and forth to the doctor with Callie, and chasing after the boys, it felt more like two months.

"Your brother Jamey is going to be in town," she continued, "and Ann is going to be here. We thought maybe we could all go down to the McNeills' beach house outside of Galveston, on Boliver Peninsula, and spend a week there. You can relax, unwind . . ."

It sounded heavenly.

"And Dad and I can take care of the kids."

Sold.

I loved the kids more than life itself, but I had to admit, even with Tinie coming in twice a week, managing all three of them on my own was a lot harder than I had expected.

"Do you think I should?" I asked Dev that night.

"Oh, I think it's a great idea," he said. "You haven't seen Jamey in ages, and a change of scenery might do you some good. Besides, it's been kind of a rough couple of months for the boys. They'd probably benefit from a few days with your mom and Doc on the beach as well."

There was no question about that. There was no such thing as too much time with my dad where the boys were concerned.

A few days later, Dev took the kids and me to the airport, walking us to the gate. He had to stay behind to catch up on work. I hadn't really stopped to think about it, but even though Dev had been back to work for six weeks, he was still catching up—though this was the first time he even mentioned needing to make up some lost time. He never complained, never said, "I can't right now," and he never made me feel as though I wasn't doing my fair share. That's just the kind of guy Dev is.

We spent almost the entire week at the beach. It was wonderful seeing Jamey again. He looked exactly the way I'd remembered him, and even though he couldn't tell us much about the work he had been doing overseas, he was able to share just enough about his "secret agent" lifestyle to thoroughly captivate Casen and Conner, who marveled at him like he was Superman, Batman, and James Bond all rolled into one.

"Those boys just idolize you," I told him one afternoon as he, Ann, and I lounged on the sand, the waves washing rhythmically over our feet.

"Not as much as they idolize Doc," Jamey said, nodding toward where Dad was building a sandcastle with Casen and Conner off in the distance. A few yards behind him, Mom was perched under an enormous umbrella, gently rocking Callie. We had barely left the airport before my parents officially took charge of the kids, giving me a welcome break and ample time to sit and visit with Ann and Jamey.

Every time I tried to help, Mom would shoo me away. "I've got

Callie," she would say. "You go sit in the sun and talk to your brother and sister. Goodness knows when we might see Jamey again." It was almost like my first week at home all over again—except this time, I remembered everything.

We had spent countless days and weeks here at the beach when I was growing up, so I knew the McNeills' beach house and this stretch of sand like the back of my hand. And reminiscing with Ann and Jamey about when we were kids made me feel like not a day had passed. It was a welcome relief from my life back in Charlotte, where everything felt foreign and everyone a stranger.

"Do you remember when Jamey left all those crabs in Dad's car?" Ann said, breaking into a wide smile.

"Remember it . . ." I said, "I swear sometimes I can still smell it!" It was hard to forget. When Jamey was little, Dad took him out crabbing, and Jamey, who had always had a soft spot for animals, wanted to save the crabs and bring them home as pets, so he hid them in Dad's car. By the time we were ready to leave four days later, they had all died and the stench was positively ungodly.

"I thought Dad was going to skin you alive," Ann snickered.

Jamey, who was reminded of this story every time we came to the beach, ate seafood, or passed a crab shack, just rolled his eyes. "How was I supposed to know crabs needed water to live?"

I laughed and tilted my head back in the sun, the cool ocean breeze blowing through my hair, which, thankfully, was filling in nicely. I could hear Casen and Conner giggling over the waves washing along the shore. It was so strange being someplace so familiar and laughing with Ann and Jamey about events from almost twenty years ago, yet still being unable to remember a thing about Casen or Conner's births or their lives before Callie. Part of me selfishly wished I could stay here forever.

"Doc's not getting much lolling time this week, is he?" Jamey smiled, watching Dad scoop up another bucket of wet sand.

I smiled. Whenever we would come to the beach as kids, Dad would spend hours camped out on the front porch of the beach house, napping and quietly watching the waves roll in—just lying around, doing nothing, or "lolling," as he called it.

"Nope," I said, feeling the slightest twinge of guilt.

"Oh, who are we kidding, they're both loving this," Ann chirped, glancing back at Mom and Callie.

She was right. "I wish we lived closer," I said, wondering why Dev and I had moved to Charlotte in the first place. I quickly shook the thought from my head. It had been far too perfect a week to let all of the confusion and chaos of the last two months seep back in and ruin it.

That night, after Mom got Callie down, I went to check on Casen and Conner. When I got to their room, the door was open, and Dad was sitting on the edge of Casen's bed, both boys' eyes glued to him.

"Tell us a story," Casen begged.

"Okay," Dad relented, "but just one. It's getting late. You boys need to get some sleep."

I chuckled to myself. If anyone needed sleep after spending the whole day building sandcastles, hunting for seashells, and chasing sandpipers up and down the beach, it was Dad.

"Once upon a time," he began, "there were two little boys named Jason and Bonner Craig, and they were *always* getting into trouble." The boys both giggled at Dad's obvious play on their names, and my heart melted right down to my toes. "One day, Jason and Bonner set out to . . ."

I stood there quietly in the doorway listening to Dad weave a masterful story about Jason and Bonner's magical kingdom made of sand and made a conscious effort to commit every last detail of the evening to memory. I had no idea how many other memories like this were now lost to me forever, but this night—in fact, this whole week—was one I was *never* going to forget.

CHAPTER 14

A
BREATH
OF HOPE

The sweltering heat of a North Carolina August beat down on my neck as I filled up the plastic swimming pool in our backyard. It was a far cry from the beach in Texas, but it was better than nothing.

The boys were up in the tree house Dev had built them, their favorite place to play, while Callie dozed in her carrier on the patio. As I watched the waterline rise, gratitude rose within me for days like this. It was these lazy afternoons playing with the kids that kept me going despite the continued confusion and frustration of constantly having to act a part in a play I had never seen the script for.

Happily, fewer and fewer people were stopping by to drop off casseroles and to "visit." It was hard making small talk with people I couldn't remember about other people and events I couldn't remember. It was so much easier just being with the kids. Casen and Conner lived so much in the moment. Rarely, if ever, did I hear either of them utter the phrase, "Mommy, do you remember . . ." And, of

117

MARCY GREGG

course, Callie was a blank slate. I may have missed out on her first two weeks of life, but we were creating new memories every day. All of us were.

"Casen, Conner, come on down, boys, the pool is ready!" I yelled as I turned off the hose. The boys scampered down the few steps from the tree house and jumped in the pool, splashing and shrieking with delight.

"Can I have a popsicle, Mama?" Casen asked, kicking his legs in the water.

"Popsicle!" Conner echoed. I had quickly learned that if Casen wanted something, Conner wanted it too.

"Okay, but you have to eat them outside," I said. I went into the kitchen, which was finally devoid of Tupperware containers and casserole dishes. God bless Dev, he had taken it upon himself to return all of them while we were in Texas last month, sparing me the embarrassment of having to confess I still couldn't place faces with names or remember where many of our friends lived. Once inside, I lingered in the chill of the now stocked-to-the-brim freezer for a few seconds as I tried to remember where I had put the popsicles. It didn't take long to realize we didn't have any. I grabbed a handful of cookies from the cookie jar—a poor substitution for a popsicle on a hot day, but it would have to do.

"Boys, I'm afraid we're all out of popsicles," I said, handing them two chocolate chip cookies each. "I have to go to the drugstore this afternoon, and we can pick some up then, okay?"

Happily, they were so busy pushing their little toy boats around in the water, the cookies seemed to suffice.

Later that afternoon, I loaded the boys and Callie in the car, letting Tinie know where we were going, and headed toward Eckerd drugstore at the Cotswold shopping center, located on one of the dreaded Sharon roads. Thankfully by now, I was able to tell Sharon, Sharon Amity, and Sharon Lane apart, and I had managed not to get lost since the equally dreaded melting ice cream incident. Other little things like writing and finding things around the house had gotten easier too. And, thankfully, pre-coma Marcy was apparently very type A and kept meticulous records of birthdays, anniversaries, addresses, and phone numbers, so I was getting a little better at managing day-to-day activities.

Still, I often felt nervous going out to run errands for fear of running into someone I couldn't remember. Just walking down the aisle of the grocery store or standing in line at the post office set the butterflies loose in my stomach as I never knew which faces I should react to and which I could just let walk by. It wasn't quite as bad when I was with Dev. I would just let him start the conversation then follow his lead. Whether he knew I still needed his prompting on names and key details, I wasn't entirely sure. I was just grateful he continued to do it. And that he never confronted me about it. No one did.

When we were in Texas, I got the sense that Mom and Dad both knew I was struggling to get a handle on things at home. Jamey's visit just proved an advantageous excuse to give me a much-needed break. But even if they did suspect, to their credit, they never said anything. You can tell a lot by a look or a glance, though.

All I ever heard from Mom and Dad was, "We're so proud of you, Marcy," and "You're doing so well." Maybe they thought their encouragement would become a self-fulfilling prophecy. It hadn't. At least not yet. But their undying support still meant the world to me.

Once we got to the mall, I found a parking space and made a mental note of where it was. We were, after all, buying more popsicles, and today was even hotter than the ice cream day. I put Callie in her stroller and carefully led the boys up the sidewalk and into the drugstore. The air-conditioning felt spectacular. Instantly rejuvenated, the boys raced down the aisle to the frozen desserts section while I stepped in line for the pharmacist, to pick up Callie's ear meds.

"Marcy, is that you?"

I turned around to see a tall, blonde woman wearing jean shorts and a T-shirt, with a baby perched on her hip. I smiled politely and racked my brain for a name.

"Yes! Hi there! How are you?" I asked, instantly feeling warmer than I should, given that the thermostat had to have been set in the low sixties.

"Pretty well, all things considered," she said. "Just trying to stay out of this heat."

"I know," I played along. "I can't remember the last time it was this hot."

"I'm so glad to see you doing so well," she said. "You look great! Dev called us every week with updates. What a horrific ordeal!" She looked genuinely sympathetic. Nice. Friendly. Like someone I would be friends with. "I'm just so glad you're okay."

I nodded and quickly pivoted to what I knew. "We were very lucky. My doctors were amazing."

"Well . . ." she said, hiking the infant up on her hip again, "the way Dev described it sounds like nothing short of a miracle. It's obvious God healed you."

I paused. He had. And yet . . .

"He's definitely answered our prayers," I finally managed. I had been in enough of these awkward conversations to know that statement typically stopped the questions. After all, what else was there to say?

The baby on her hip started to fuss, thankfully, drawing the attention off of me. "This one has just not been sleeping well," she said, bouncing the child up and down a bit. "Did you have this much trouble when your kids were teething?"

I smiled weakly. "Oh, they struggled to sleep through the night. Thankfully it was just a phase." I had no idea how Conner or Casen had slept as babies or what their teething was like, but again, it seemed like the easiest way to end this conversation.

Her baby started to whimper. "Well, it was great to run into you, Marcy." She smiled. "Maybe we'll see you and Dev at church sometime!"

Church. It was the only context clue I picked up during our brief yet interminable exchange.

Callie's medicine in hand, I paid for the boys' popsicles and hurried them back to the car before we could run into anyone else. For a big city, Charlotte was proving to be an awfully small town.

As I drove home, I prayed:

Lord, please let my memories come back. Even if it's only a few. It's just so painful to be reminded every day of everything I've lost. I'm so tired of pretending, but everyone already treats me as though I'm so fragile, I might break at any moment. How will they treat me if they find out the truth? Besides, I've been faking it for so long now, I don't even know how I could tell people the truth. *I seem to have gotten myself into a bit of a bind, and I don't know who else to turn to but you, Lord. I know you can heal me because you did it before. Please . . . I'm asking you, heal me again.*

When I got home from the pharmacy, Tinie was there, waiting to make sure we got home okay. The boys ran to give her a hug, and she took Callie out of my arms with a smile.

After I unloaded the bags, I came in and found Tinie was sitting on the sofa rocking a dozing Callie. I watched for a moment, the same sadness I'd felt on our drive home welling up in my heart. Tinie was such a big part of our lives, yet I couldn't even remember our first meeting.

I sat down next to her and said, "Tell me about when you first came to our family."

Tinie smiled at the memory. "The first time I met you, you walked into the room with Conner on your hip. He had these big brown eyes; he looked just like you. We hit it off immediately."

"How soon did you start to work for us?" I asked.

"Right away," Tinie said. "For me, it was love at first sight for your boys, and it's always been that way. We were in your other house at that time, of course, right after you moved to Charlotte."

"Tell me about those days," I said. I had seen pictures of me and the boys at that house, a red brick two-story with a woodsy backyard.

Tinie laughed. "We had lots of fun together. But one day I was keeping the boys while you were out, and Casen climbed up the apple tree and got stuck. He was only four years old then. I couldn't believe he had gotten up that high."

Even though the danger was already over, I still felt a twinge of fear for my intrepid Casen. "What did you do?" I asked.

"I climbed the tree!" she exclaimed. "What anyone would do. He was fifteen feet in the air. I just held that boy tight and brought him down. Then we ate an apple together." She laughed at the memory. "He wasn't fazed at all."

"I would do anything for those boys," Tinie continued. She looked down at Callie, sleeping in her arms. "And now we've got our baby girl, too."

Listening to Tinie talk, my heart swelled. I was so grateful for Tinie, for the love she clearly had for my sons and daughter. Yet I also grieved for the memories I had lost, for the things she knew about them that I couldn't remember.

She put an arm around me and squeezed us close. "I'll always be there for the children," she said. "You know I love them like my own."

~

The next day, Lamentations 3:22-23 kept returning to my mind: *His compassions never fail. They are new every morning; great is your faithfulness.* As I picked up school supplies for Casen and got dinner ready, I held a glimmer of hope that God would answer my prayers.

Maybe I could do something to help trigger the memories.

I flashed back to my first day home from the hospital. There was something about our bedroom that felt familiar. It was the scent of my perfume, Anais Anais. I hadn't been able to place it at first, but when I saw the bottle on the dresser, it was like *I knew.* And the colors in Callie's nursery had also felt familiar—mint green and pale pink—as though I remembered picking them out.

That night, after the kids were in bed and Dev was watching a golf tournament on TV, I gingerly opened the door in the kitchen that led up to the attic. The smell of dust and mothballs wafted down.

I slowly walked up the stairs. The attic spanned the length of our house. It was full of storage boxes, heirlooms, old clothes—a lifetime of memories—just none of them mine.

After checking the labels on several boxes, I finally found the box I was looking for. It was simply marked "BABY."

Please, Lord . . . please let this work.

Opening the top of the box like a gift, I reached down and pulled out a large stack of onesies, bibs, and blankets in various shades of pale blue and mint green. They were soft to the touch like old flannel. There was a tiny sweatshirt with a truck printed on the front and a wool sweater with a Christmas tree stitched to the front. Farther down in the box were some old wooden toys and a stuffed bear, its ears worn down to the fabric underneath.

I grabbed a handful of clothes up to my nose, buried my face in them, and inhaled deeply.

Please come back . . . please let the memories of my children come back.

Nothing.

I took another deep breath, this time rubbing the softened fabric against my cheek, willing an image from the past to emerge from the fog of my brain.

Just one memory of bringing Casen home from the hospital . . . or giving a bottle to Conner . . . or Casen reaching for me from his crib . . . or bathing them . . . anything, Lord. Please.

But no matter how fervently I rubbed that fabric against my skin or tried to breathe in the undeniable scent of "baby boy," I couldn't retrieve a single moment. Tears burning the backs of my eyes, I stuffed the clothes and the bear back in the box and hastily folded it shut. As I descended the stairs into the kitchen, I caught sight of the pictures on our refrigerator. They were the same ones Dev had taped to my hospital bed. I pinched the bridge of my nose in frustration as the tears threatened to fall. I could still smell the baby clothes on my hands. I looked up at the photos and sniffed my fingers one last time. *Maybe together . . .*

Nothing. I leaned back on the counter and the tears began to fall as the stark realization settled over me . . .

The memories are gone.

Forever.

PART 3

DRINKING
TO
FORGET

CHAPTER 15

JUST GETTING THROUGH THE DAY

OCTOBER 1990

"Okay, Casen, try reading the problem out loud again."

I stared down at the first-grade math workbook open in front of us at the kitchen table. Ever since Casen had returned to school a few weeks ago, I dreaded homework hour. Sometimes it felt like my seven-year-old was better at math than I was. According to Dev, who had noticed me struggling to balance the checkbook a few weeks ago, numbers had never been my forte. He said I'd always been more of a creative. I *did* love coloring with the boys. Sometimes we would sit at the kitchen table together for hours with a box of crayons creating to our hearts' content. Still, to not be able to think my way through a first-grade word problem made me wonder just how much damage that coma had done.

The drive from the grocery store had gotten easier, and I was now able to transport our groceries home without getting lost. Granted, a few weeks ago I drove off before the bagger had loaded the groceries into the car. I was halfway home before Casen pointed it out. I had also managed to cook a few decent meals, thanks in large part to Mom, who sent me foolproof recipes for a delicious chicken casserole, a great pork chop recipe, and, Dev's favorite, her famous apple pie.

I had a handful of friends I saw regularly, and the number of faces I could match to names was growing, but our conversations felt superficial, limited to things I could speak to with some confidence, such as things I had learned secondhand from Dev. While I was grateful for the friendships, I hated that they were all so one-sided. I wanted to get to know them better, but after the adoption slipup with Holly in the hospital, I was afraid to ask anyone something I should already have known.

Tinie was still coming to help around the house, though only once a week at this point. But beyond the day-to-day chores and mothering duties, the hardest thing was how exhausted I felt from the effort of putting on a good face each day, pretending I had it all together, while my brain was straining for knowledge or skills I should already have had. I didn't want anyone to know how much of a struggle these seemingly simple tasks were for me—so I kept it all inside.

Before the episode in the attic, I had held out some hope that my long-term memories would come back, but now, my morning prayers were all punctuated with a tinge of complaint:

Lord, why didn't you heal me completely?

Why did you save my life only to have me awake to this mess?

You say all things work for good for those who know and love you, but what good could possibly come from me not remembering my own children's lives?

"Mom," Casen looked up at me, clearly frustrated. "I'm tired of thinking. Can we stop now?"

I ran my fingers through his hair. Poor little guy. I knew exactly how he felt.

⌒

"I don't know any moms who don't struggle, Marcy," my friend assured me.

Of course, I was betting most of them remembered their kids' first words, steps, and birthday parties. Still, it was nice to hear someone else admit they didn't quite have it all together. It had taken me weeks to get up the nerve to admit to anyone I was struggling. Today, however, had pushed me to my breaking point. I had barely made it through another disheartening homework session with Casen; Callie, who was battling her third ear infection in as many weeks, hadn't slept a wink the night before and had been fussy all day; and Conner . . . well, Conner was being a typical three-year-old, constantly clinging to my legs, begging for attention and energy I simply didn't have to give.

"I'm glad I'm not the only one," I said, as I tried, in vain, to scrub a swath of petrified grape jelly off the countertop. "How do you manage it all?"

"Honestly," she laughed, "I usually have a glass of wine. It's my reward for getting through the day."

A glass of wine . . . the idea was novel. Truthfully, I couldn't remember ever drinking, although we did have a full complement of wine glasses and beer mugs in the house.

"Everyone I know struggles around five o'clock," she continued. "I find a nice glass of chardonnay while I'm preparing dinner helps take the edge off."

I definitely felt edgy. Playdates, doctor's appointments, car pools, homework, housework, the boys' lunches, Dev's dinner, Callie's medication—I felt like I was on a merry-go-round that kept spinning faster and faster, and I couldn't get off.

My friend's words echoed in my head all night and well into the next morning. After lunch, while Tinie went to pick up the boys from soccer and a playdate, I loaded the dishwasher, changed Callie into a clean outfit, put her in her car seat, and drove out to Harris Teeter, where I made my way to one of the back aisles.

I didn't know anything about wine. I glanced at the different labels. *Cabernet? Pinot Grigio? Riesling? What's the difference?*

Callie was starting to fuss, so I grabbed a bottle with a hand-drawn gold leaf on the label and read the description: "hints of pear and apple with delicate floral notes and a light crisp finish."

I *did* like pears and apples. And the label was certainly pretty.

I slipped the bottle under my free arm and made my way to the checkout line, feeling slightly self-conscious but not sure why.

She did say everyone does it, I reminded myself. And for once, I just wanted to be like everyone else.

My "reward for a hard day" in hand, Callie and I made our way back outside. I put the paper bag on the passenger side floor next to Casen's soccer ball and a half-empty package of baby wipes, loaded Callie into her car seat, and headed for home. The crisp fall air carried the scent of burning leaves. Once we got home, I stuck the bottle in the cabinet next to the fridge, behind a row of cereal boxes.

"There you are!"

I quickly shut the cabinet and spun around to find Tinie smiling at me from the other side of the room.

My mind started to race. *How long has she been standing there? Did she see my hiding the bottle?*

"I was *wondering* where you'd gone."

"Oh, Callie and I just went out for a little drive," I said, carefully positioning myself directly in front of the cabinet.

"Beautiful day for it," she said. "I picked Casen up from soccer practice and Conner up from his playdate. I told them they could play outside till supper."

As if on cue, Casen came tearing through the kitchen on his way to the back door, Conner fast on his heels.

"Casen and Conner Gregg," Tinie said sternly. "Do you not see your mama standing there?"

The boys froze, Casen's hand still on the doorknob, their eyes on Tinie.

"Hi, Mommy," Conner offered up, flashing me a huge smile.

"Hi, Mom," Casen chirped, his eyes quickly darting from me back to Tinie.

"That's better," Tinie said. "Go ahead then," she shooed them out the door. "Honestly . . . those boys," she sighed, a smile crossing her own face. She absolutely adored Casen and Conner, and the feeling was mutual. She would spend hours playing with them in their little tree house fort, take them to the park to burn off extra energy on the jungle gym, and whenever Conner would get antsy while I was helping Casen with his homework, she would take him outside and push him up and down the driveway in his Little Tikes car until Dev got home. Whenever Tinie was there, those boys' hands were always clean, their hair was always combed, and they never sat down to an afternoon snack without bowing their heads and thanking Jesus first. I had no idea what I would do without her.

"Would you like me to take this little one?" she asked, reaching for Callie.

"That would be wonderful," I said, handing her over. "Thank you, Tinie."

"I'll just get her down for a nap," she said, cradling Callie in her arms.

"Good luck," I said. "She's been fussy all week."

"You just leave that to me," she said, kissing the top of Callie's head.

As soon as they were out of sight, I opened the cabinet again, moved the boxes aside, pushed the bottle as far back as it would go, then rearranged the boxes to make doubly sure nobody could see it.

I probably won't even touch it, I mused, turning my attention to dinner. Twenty minutes later, I had a large pot of spaghetti boiling away on the stove, a smaller pot of sauce just starting to bubble, and a loaf of garlic bread heating up in the oven.

Tinie came out of the bedroom as I was stirring the sauce.

"How's Callie?" I asked.

"Restless." She took the spoon out of my hand. "I'll take care of this, Marcy. You just go check on Callie. I think she's still running a little bit of a fever."

I exhaled about seven months' worth of stress and headed toward the nursery to check on Callie.

Inside the nursery I closed the door behind me. Callie was fussing and moving about a little in her crib, but one look also told me that she had just about worn herself out.

"How are you feeling, sweetie?" I asked, gently resting the back of my hand against her forehead. Tinie was right. She felt warm. I picked her up, carried her over to the rocking chair in the corner, sat down, and slowly began rocking her, my heart still fluttering like a hummingbird.

She looked up at me, cooed, yawned, then closed her eyes and drifted off to sleep.

I had never been so envious of anyone in my life.

"You okay?" Dev asked as we cleared the table.

I took a deep breath and sighed. "I'll be fine. It's just . . . Callie's been fussy. And helping Casen with his homework is a lot sometimes." *And I'm just so tired of everything that should be simple feeling hard.*

"You're doing great," Dev encouraged me.

Tinie had told me almost the same thing before she left. "Marcy," she said, holding my arms and staring me straight in the eyes, "you're a good mama."

Was I?

"I'm going to catch the end of the golf tournament on TV," Dev said, placing the last of the dishes in the dishwasher. "Want to join me?"

"No, I'm pretty tired. I'm probably just going to head to bed."

"Okay." He kissed me on the cheek. "Dinner tonight was great, by the way."

God bless that man. How many times in the past seven months had he come home to a messy kitchen and me trying to salvage a meal I'd let cook a little too long? Or found me near tears trying to figure out Casen's word problems? And yet he always had something positive to say. Where he found his optimism, I had no idea. After today, mine was sorely lacking.

I finished wiping down the countertop, and then I turned and looked at the cabinet.

Hints of pear and apple with delicate floral notes . . .

I left the kitchen and went down the hall. The boys' room and Callie's nursery were both silent and dark. Dev and I had put the kids to bed right after supper. It was a little earlier than the boys' usual bedtime, but they were both so wound up from the afternoon, Dev thought it would probably do my nervous system a world of good if they turned in early. Farther down the hall, the light from the TV and the sound of the announcer were the only signs of life in an otherwise silent house.

Going back to the kitchen, I opened the cabinet and dug the bottle out from behind the cereal boxes. I grabbed a wine glass from the back of the china cabinet and rummaged around the junk drawer until I found a corkscrew. After rinsing a thin coating of dust from the bottom of the glass, I uncorked the bottle and took a sniff. A sweet, crisp acidity filled my nose.

I poured until the glass was full, stuck the cork back in the bottle, and quickly stashed it back in the cabinet. I swirled the wine around in the glass, watching it shimmer under the light from the kitchen.

I brought the glass to my lips and took a sip. Almost instantly, liquid warmth radiated throughout my entire body. After a few more sips, my head felt like it was floating a few inches above my neck, and the knot that had formed in the pit of my stomach throughout the day loosened.

Wow . . . she wasn't kidding . . . I already feel better.

I took another sip, and the warm glow reached all the way to my toes. The effects were immediate. A few more sips and I was floating.

Now I know why so many moms end the day like this . . .

Before I knew it, the glass was empty. I opened the cabinet again and reached up for the bottle, then froze.

Be careful.

Despite my friend's assurance that this was perfectly normal, I had to admit, it felt very much out of the ordinary. How many times had I heard Tinie caution the boys, "If you're afraid of getting caught, you probably shouldn't be doing it."

But I wasn't a little child. I was a grown woman. A grown woman who had lost thirteen years' worth of memories—marriage, kids, vacations, holidays, family gatherings, friends—all gone, erased like chalk on a blackboard. If *anyone* deserved a break . . .

I stood there for several minutes, deliberating, the faint sounds of the TV barely discernible in the distance. As I turned to look out the window, I caught a glimpse of my Bible sitting on the counter next to the phone. I had left it there after my morning prayer time.

Lord— I closed my eyes. *I have prayed and prayed that my memory would come back. I have begged. I have pleaded. But nothing has changed. Nothing has come back. Not my college years, not my wedding, the birth of my children, my friends, anything. My mind feels almost as muddled as it did the day I woke up. Are you even listening? More and more it's starting to feel as though you've left me to fend for myself.*

I opened my eyes, facing the refrigerator. It was covered in the photos of the kids Dev had brought to the hospital. I had left them up in hopes that one day I might remember the story behind one of them, but they were as foreign to me today as they were the day Dev and the nurse taped them to my bed.

Lord, I muttered, pouring a second glass, *you can run the universe. I will handle my world.*

CHAPTER 16

CHRISTMAS CARDS

DECEMBER 1990

The twinkling lights and ornaments on the Christmas tree filled the living room with a shimmering glow. At the base of the tree were the kids' presents I had bought and wrapped the week prior. The needle-point stockings from Mom were hung on the mantel, with Callie's as the newest addition, every stitch sewn with care and love. Looking around the room on a chilly December evening, I swelled with pride that I had managed to get the house ready for the first Christmas I could remember as an adult.

I took a sip of chardonnay, and Dev sat down on the couch and put his arm around my shoulder.

"The tree looks beautiful, Marcy. You've put all the decorations together perfectly." He sighed deeply. "What a year we've had."

That was the understatement of the century.

I rested my head on his shoulder.

"I thought maybe we could look at these together," he said, holding up a stack of red and green envelopes.

Oh no . . . not this again.

Every day for the past two weeks, cards had been appearing in the mailbox, postmarked from places far and wide, wishing the Greggs warm holiday cheer and regaling us with stories from everyone's year. After the kids were down for the evening, I'd sit at the kitchen table and open a card, admiring the angels and poinsettias artfully rendered on the front before trying to follow our friends' stories about kids, jobs, and vacations. Most of the cards included a note about the coma and prayers for a better year than 1990 had been. While sweet, every card was nonetheless a sinking reminder of everything I had lost.

"It looks like this one's from Margie and Neil," said Dev as he tore open the top of the envelope. I peeked over his shoulder as he scanned the typed note tucked into the card, glancing past the text to the photo at the bottom to see if the smiling faces staring back at me looked at all familiar. They were like faces from a dream. There was something distantly familiar about their features, but any memory of my friendship with them—how and where we met and things we had done together—was gone.

Dev paused before opening the next card in the stack. "Oh, this one's from Jahn and Gregg."

I leaned farther into Dev. "How are they?"

"Good," he said, reading the letter. "Oh, what a nice photo of the kids." He held up a photo of a happy, smiling family. "They're getting so big, aren't they?" He looked at me, and I nodded, taking a sip of wine to avoid having to say anything further. Dev's tone grew sentimental. "I miss our old Dallas Bible study friends, don't you?"

I took another sip, emptying my glass, and Dev's brow furrowed.

"Marcy . . . are you okay?"

I swallowed hard. Should I tell him the truth? That I don't remember any of these people? That I've been covering—and lying—all this time?

"Dev . . ." The words caught in my throat as my eyes welled up.

Dev put the card down and took my hand in his. "What is it, sweetheart?"

A sob emerged from my chest. "I'm trying so hard to remember, but . . . Dev, it's not coming back. None of it is."

"Oh, Marcy." He cupped my cheek in his hand. "Why didn't you say something sooner?"

I wiped away a tear. "I've just been so scared. I pray every morning for God to heal me, but my mind still feels so jumbled."

"Marcy," Dev quickly cut me off. "It's okay. It's going to be okay. You've been doing so well. Taking care of the kids . . . and me. The doctors said your old memories would come back over time. We have to keep trusting that they were right. We just have to wait."

"I'm trying so hard, Dev. I want so badly to believe that God is hearing my prayers and that he'll answer them, but to trust that God hears my prayers . . ." I rested my head in my hands. "I just thought my memories would have come back by now."

Dev gently rubbed my back. "Marcy, don't expect too much too fast. We haven't seen some of these people in years. It's understandable if you can't remember them right away."

That's when it hit me. Dev didn't know. He just thought I was having trouble remembering our old friends and the occasional well-wisher from church. He had no idea I had also forgotten us—our college years, our engagement story, our wedding, moving to Charlotte, having the boys, Callie's birth . . .

I looked at Dev's face. He already looked so forlorn. Did I dare tell him the extent of my memory problems?

Just tell him, Marcy . . .

I opened my mouth, but the mere thought of disrupting the life we were just starting to piece together with a possible trip back to the hospital for more tests or more rehab stopped me.

After a few silent moments, Dev rested his hand on my back, lowered his head, and began to pray:

"Lord, we ask you to give Marcy back the memories that are still lost to her. Please bring healing to her, Lord. We're so grateful that she's alive and back home with us. Please help her to remember our friends. Help her to remember all the good times we've had together. The relationships we've forged. The people who care about her. Help her, Lord. In your Son's name we pray."

Dev squeezed my hand, and without even thinking about it, I said, "Amen."

But my eyes were on the glass in my hands.

Between March and December, I'd finally formed a core group of friends I felt comfortable being around, but our circles grew larger over the holidays. Dev and I were invited to Christmas parties, and the kids had school events I was expected to attend. Everywhere I went were faces I didn't recognize, people who knew me, who thought I was better, fully recovered from my coma. I smiled, I laughed, I chatted—about the weather and holiday plans and favorite recipes and what the kids wanted for Christmas.

The chore of buying Christmas presents—for the kids, for extended family members, for neighbors—wasn't easy, either. To say I was stressed would be an understatement.

Somehow, I made it through the holiday season, with all the parties and gatherings it entailed, but by the time January rolled around, I was exhausted from putting on a good front. As the days went on, it just got easier and easier at the end of the day to open the cupboard and reach for the bottle hidden behind the cereal boxes.

CHAPTER 17

THE
DINNER
PARTY

SPRING 1991

"Okay, boys, you be on your best behavior for Dena tonight." I
crouched down and kissed each of them on the cheek.

"We will, Mom," Casen assured me.

"Don't you worry about a thing," Dena said. "You just enjoy your
night out." She was holding onto Callie's tiny hands, helping her to
balance. Ever since Callie'd had her corrective surgery a few months
ago, she had been like a different baby—sleeping through the night,
smiling and laughing more, and eager as all get-out to start moving
around on her own. Still, every little milestone we celebrated together
was one more reminder of similar moments with the boys that had
been lost to me forever.

"Thanks, Dena." I smiled as Dev pulled up our Volvo station
wagon. "We will."

Truth be told, I had been nervous about this evening ever since Dev first mentioned it. We had been invited to dinner with some old friends from years back. Dev had recently run into the husband, and the evening was planned. I wasn't sure who would be there, if I would remember any of them, or how I would manage any conversation that went beyond, "How have you been?" but Dev was understandably anxious to get back into our old social circles, and I didn't want him to have to miss out on anything because of me. Besides, since my partial confession at Christmas, I knew Dev would be watching me closely in the event that I needed either a prompt or a full-on rescue.

Dev and I wound our way through residential streets until we pulled into the driveway of our host's home. The front door opened and a man wearing khakis and a blue polo shirt smiled and waved us in.

"You okay?" Dev reached for my hand.

"Of course," I assured him. I could already feel the butterflies taking flight in the pit of my stomach.

Once in the house, we stepped into a crowd of couples talking and laughing in the kitchen. The countertops were covered in trays of freshly grilled hamburgers, deviled eggs, potato chips, and pasta salad. I set down the apple pie I had made that morning and carefully peeled the foil off the top.

"Marcy, Dev!" A woman wearing a pretty floral sundress beamed at us from across the room. "It's so good to see you after all these months!"

She rushed over and gave me a hug. I glanced over her shoulder at Dev, who mouthed, "Elizabeth."

"Thanks so much for having us, Elizabeth," I said as she pulled away. "How are you?"

"We're doing great," she gushed. "We're heading out to Pawleys Island next week with the kids."

"Oh, that sounds like fun! How *are* the kids?" I asked, hoping she'd drop a few names and helpful details.

"Oh, they're doing well—busy as ever."

I bit the inside of my cheek. That didn't help at all. *Busy with what? T-ball or studying for their SATs?*

I looked over to Dev for a little help, but he was busy talking with somebody else a few feet away. I was on my own.

"That's nice," I offered, suddenly uncertain of the last thing she'd said.

"Of course they're excited to play with their cousins," she said matter-of-factly.

That helped a little bit. Obviously the kids were younger. I didn't recognize her or the house from any playdates, so they had to be at least a little older than Conner and Casen. But how many were there? Two? Three? I glanced behind me again. Dev was still talking. This was going to be a long evening.

She reached into the fridge and pulled out a pitcher filled with fruit floating in a dark crimson liquid. "Would you like some sangria, Marcy?"

Then again . . .

"I would *love* some, thank you."

She handed me the glass, and I brought it up to my nose, taking in the familiar fruity aroma. Over the past several months, I had become something of a connoisseur, frequenting the back aisle of Harris Teeter two or sometimes three times a week. I never bought more than two bottles at a time, lest it arouse suspicion. As I quickly discovered that wine tasted better cold, I had taken to keeping one bottle in the fridge and hiding another in the pantry at all times, replacing the one in the fridge when empty, and burying the empties in the trash, so Dev wouldn't be able to tell how quickly we were going through them.

On occasion, he'd even have a glass with me. Though Dev usually stopped at one, most nights I found myself reaching for a second and third—one with Dev, and then two more later, after Dev had gone to bed.

It had become a quiet, careful ritual: after Dev had turned in and the house was quiet, I'd get the corkscrew from the drawer, take a glass from the cabinet, open a fresh bottle, and within minutes, all the mental confusion, frustration, and fatigue of the day would evaporate like little puffs of smoke. The tension in my neck and back would ease, and I'd be filled with renewed confidence that I could make it through another day of meal preparation, math homework, cartoons, and car pools.

Granted, sometimes the next morning started out a bit rough. I'd open my eyes and feel the strain of a headache, regretting that I hadn't stopped after the second glass the night before. Each morning, before the kids were up, I'd start my devotions at the kitchen table the same as I always did: with a cup of coffee and my Bible. But now my prayers were tinged with guilt.

I overdid it last night, Lord. I'm sorry. I'm going to stop for a while . . . take a break. I don't like waking up like this, feeling tired and foggy as I go about the day taking care of the kids. I don't want it to distract from my time with them.

Yet despite the promises made in morning prayer, in truth, I was neither ready nor able to stop.

As the sangria coursed warmly through my veins, I felt a welcome burst of confidence in this room full of friends-turned-strangers. And for once . . . I didn't have to hide it.

After enduring what felt like hours of arduous small talk about summer vacations and sports camps, Elizabeth's husband, Michael, called out, "Okay, everyone, head to the living room!"

We meandered down the hallway to a large den with a beautifully covered sofa and two club chairs that I loved, family photos on the walls, and music playing from a stereo in the bookcases.

"Oh, this takes me back!" said one of the men as everyone found a seat. "Honey, remember when we went to see Bruce Springsteen on the Born in the U.S.A. tour? They don't call him The Boss for nothing!"

"My favorite concert was the Allman Brothers, at the Greensboro Coliseum back in 1981," one of the other guests said wistfully as he scanned the husband's CD collection. "They played for three hours that night. Remember?"

"Yes, I remember you dragged me to it on one of our first dates!" his wife said, chuckling. "It was a bit loud for my taste." Some of the other wives nodded knowingly.

"You know what?" one of the other women suggested eagerly. "Everyone should go around the room and say what their first concert was!"

Oh no . . .

Anxiety bubbled up inside my chest as people went around the room, regaling the group with stories of Elton John's crazy outfits, Billy Joel's encore of "Piano Man," the ear-piercing guitar riffs of Guns N' Roses, and a whole score of musicians I had never heard of. Honestly, not remembering which bands I liked in my twenties was probably the least of my losses, but as the group continued to share their favorite pop culture moments, I realized I couldn't connect with them on any of the music, movies, or books that had come out in the last decade. It was like I was from a different era; a whole chapter of shared cultural memory was lost to me and made me feel on the outside of the circle.

"What about you, Marcy?"

I looked around the room, then over at Dev, who gave me a reassuring glance.

First concert . . . The only concert I could remember was the summer before SMU . . . I was seventeen . . . I was in Dallas . . . James Taylor. That's it! James Taylor?!

"I'm pretty sure it was James Taylor, the summer before college," I said hesitantly.

145

Someone started humming the chorus of "Fire and Rain," as I looked at Dev to see if that had landed, and he nodded and winked as if to say, "I'll take it from here."

"It couldn't have been better than the Jimmy Buffett concert we saw our senior year at SMU," he said, squeezing my shoulder.

A few folks started singing, "Wastin' away again in Margaritaville / Searchin' for my lost shaker of salt . . ."

"That would have been a few months before we got engaged," Dev continued.

"Where did you go on your honeymoon?" one of the women asked.

I took another sip of sangria and looked at Dev, hoping he'd answer on our behalf. Even if he didn't know just how much I didn't remember, he at least knew some of the details were fuzzy—and that the last thing I wanted was to embarrass myself in a room full of friends who had no idea anything was wrong.

Dev looked at me for a beat before answering. "We went to Paradise Island in the Bahamas. We were so exhausted after the wedding, I don't think we moved off our beach towels the whole week!"

As Dev continued to describe the honeymoon I may as well not even have been on, I drained the last of my sangria, staring in disappointment as the ice cubes rattled at the bottom of the empty glass. I kept my eyes down, trying to stop the welling sadness from spilling out in front of the group.

Several hours and sangrias later, Dev and I finally said our goodbyes and left. It had been a long night. I was fairly certain I didn't make any significant slipups, though to be honest, the entire night felt a little hazy.

Dev unlocked the car, and I plopped down into the passenger's seat, my legs feeling decidedly more wobbly than when we had arrived. I rolled the window down, hoping the crisp night air would sharpen my senses a little.

"Did you have a good time?" Dev asked as he pulled out into traffic.

I nodded solemnly. "I just wish I could have remembered a few more details about everyone's families." I paused for a second. "And about our time at SMU." I held my breath for a moment, wondering if I had just let a little too much info slip out.

Dev just chuckled. "Heck, I don't remember everything from back then. College feels like such a long time ago."

Whether he missed the implication or was just being gallant, I couldn't tell. Either way, I breathed a sigh of relief. I had made it through the evening without making any major mistakes. That was all that mattered.

We rode in silence for a few more minutes, then Dev said, "I still pray for your memories to come back. We just have to believe that God will heal you." He reached over and took my hand. "In *his* time, Marcy. That's all we *can* do."

I nodded and stared out the window. Dev's faith felt so much stronger than mine. I had stopped asking God to bring my memories back months ago. Any and all attempts to keep hope alive just felt empty, like a well I kept trying to draw water from that had long since run dry.

After we got home, Dena had left, and Dev had climbed into bed, I put on my robe and quietly walked through each room of the house, turning off lights and putting away the toys the boys had scattered on the living room floor. I still felt a bit light-headed and wondered just how many sangrias I had had that evening.

As I walked toward the bedroom, my body was practically screaming at me to lie down, yet something drew me back to the kitchen. I turned on the light and carefully removed the bottle of pinot grigio from the fridge door so it wouldn't clink the other bottles and wake Dev. I took a glass down from the cabinet and poured until it was full. When I looked up, I caught my reflection in the window. It was well after midnight. I was wearing my bathrobe and holding a glass of wine.

"Look at yourself, Marcy," I whispered. "You just spent the entire night downing sangrias. Your legs barely got you to the car, and now you're ending the night drinking even more, all by yourself, after everyone's gone to bed. What are you doing?"

That was the problem.

I had no idea.

CHAPTER 18

GRIEVING IN A BOTTLE

MARCH 1995, FIVE YEARS AFTER THE COMA

I opened my eyes. Pain radiated around my skull and neck. A splitting pain like I hadn't felt in a long time.

Slowly turning to the left, I reached for the glass on the bedside table, gulping down the last drops of stale water. The digital clock flashed 5:43 a.m. Dev was fast asleep next to me, his chest rising and falling slowly beneath the comforter. I lay back down and rested the back of my hand against my forehead.

Maybe I'm coming down with something . . .

Just then, a flash of memory. I'm walking by tables filled with couples in a dimly lit restaurant, hoping they don't notice me struggling to walk straight. I wander down a hallway, and a waitress points me to the bathroom. Inside, the room smells like perfume and disinfectant. My stomach churns from hunger and mild nausea. I'm

149

leaning over the bathroom sink, staring in the mirror, trying to set myself straight. I examine my face, my eyes, my black cocktail dress, the gold bracelet on my wrist.

"Marcy, you are so messed up," I say to the woman in the mirror. She looks confused. Pale. Scared. Weak. I want to reach through the mirror and shake her for getting us into this mess.

I slowly sat up in bed, stretching my neck from side to side, my head heavy like a bowling ball. The light streaming in from the window revealed the outline of a dress lying rumpled across the back of a chair in the corner; black strappy heels lay askew on the floor next to it.

After unscrewing the Tylenol bottle sitting on the dresser and emptying four into my hand, I picked up the empty glass and walked down the hallway to the kitchen to fill it with cold water.

Another memory: there's a beautiful etched wine glass on a long table in front of me. All around the table are people, mostly men, chatting and laughing. I don't recognize any of them except for Dev, who is seated next to me. He's chatting and laughing too; he seems to be having a great time. I keep smiling and laughing, even though the conversation is a bit hard to follow. So many faces and names to keep track of. Every time I look down, the wine glass is filled to the brim. A waiter must be coming around to fill it, but I'm so focused on what's inside the glass, I don't notice how often it's getting filled. Nor do I really care. It makes me feel calm. Secure. Confident at this table full of strangers. It makes me feel good.

Then suddenly, I *don't* feel good. I stand up from the table; the room starts to spiral. I suddenly realize not a crumb of food has been served, only bottomless glasses of wine.

I walk away from the table in search of the bathroom, hoping my legs don't look as wobbly as they feel.

Then, a third, brief memory: I'm standing in our kitchen, getting ready to head out to the restaurant with Dev. The babysitter will be here any minute. I feel a bit on edge. The dinner is with some important clients of Dev's. He's told me their names, but I'm worried I'll mix them up. Frazzled, I look on top of the fridge, relieved to see a bottle of pinot grigio.

I rummage through the cabinet of plastic cups until I find one that's opaque and pour the contents of the bottle in. Then I take a sip.

Shaking the memory off, I headed toward the door. I needed some fresh air. As my hand hit the knob, I caught my reflection in the window. My hair was tangled; dark rings like mascara hung under my eyes.

Marcy, you are so messed up.

I felt hungry, but the thought of food made my stomach churn. I turned on the coffee maker and rested my hands on the counter, my head swimming with the realization that large swaths of the night before were gone. I couldn't remember leaving the restaurant, getting undressed, changing into my pajamas, or climbing into bed.

Dev must have helped me. I was guessing he was also the one who had left the water and the Tylenol by the bed. I felt sick. Dev must have seen me that way. What if I said something embarrassing in front of his clients? Did I stumble out to the car? Does he know how much I had to drink? How much I *had* been drinking?

I sat down at the kitchen table and racked my brain for answers that refused to come.

Of course, by now, I was used to memory loss. It had been five years since I first came home from the hospital, and despite countless trips to the attic to flip through photo albums and smell old clothes and multiple sessions with a trauma psychologist who did little more than empathize and suggest I have further testing done, the first thirteen years of Dev's and my life together were still a mystery. I had even stopped asking God for healing. What was the point? All it did was sustain false hope. Instead, I just focused on trying to create a normal life with Dev and the kids.

On this particular morning, however, I couldn't blame the coma for my memory loss. As scary as it was to admit . . . this time, I had only myself to blame.

I couldn't remember the last day I hadn't had a drink. Cravings would take over at rather inconvenient times: at Callie's dance recitals, at coffee hour after church on Sundays, even during the consulting seminars that I had started teaching at a corporate bank several months ago. My short-term memory had improved to the point where I was able to effectively write curriculum and give motivational speeches to groups as large as fifty. Still, I knew I'd be even sharper if I weren't constantly looking ahead to my next glass of wine *while* I was giving a motivational speech. And no, the irony was not lost on me. The simultaneous beauty and horror of it all was that none of my clients, colleagues, friends, or family knew just how much I relied on it.

Alcohol was like a secret friend—someone who could pat me on the back after another long day of car pools and casseroles; a buddy at parties and events where I felt left out of the group; a companion amid the loneliness created by the fact that I was still "faking fine" with so many people.

Only, as I sat there at the kitchen table, it dawned on me that alcohol had recently felt less like a friend and more like a monster who demanded to be fed. It woke me most mornings with a pounding head, mocking the fact that I had to cook breakfast, pack the kids' lunches, drive them to school, and head in for work, all with a smile. It yelled "more!" when everyone else had stopped drinking for the night. Without it, I felt irritable and restless. And now, it was robbing me of memories—and I wasn't someone who could afford to lose many more.

In the harsh morning light, I had to acknowledge that I was grieving in a bottle. That the lost memories from the coma, and this now-daily dependence on alcohol, were intertwined. More than a friend or a monster, the alcohol was a salve, even though it always wore off and made me feel even worse. Still, at the end of the day, it numbed me from the gaping loss of life that I couldn't recover and probably never would.

In a cruel twist of irony, I realized I drank to forget what I couldn't remember.

Opening my prayer journal to a fresh page, I was gripped by remorse for not listening to that gentle voice five years ago. The one that had cautioned me to *be careful*. The decision to block God out had led me to a dark, dark place. As it turned out, I wasn't very good at managing my own world after all. Last night was proof of that.

Lord, I wrote, *I'm done with the drinking. No more. I'm sorry for disobeying you . . . for not trusting you all those years ago. I now see you were trying to protect me. I see that over time, alcohol has taken more and more from me: most of all, it has taken away my intimacy with you. I suppose that's what idols do: they promise so much at first, and over time, they rob us of all that helps us flourish. So that's it. I'm giving up alcohol for good, Lord. I don't want to wake up not remembering the night before ever again. Please, Lord, give me the strength to choose a new path . . . your path.*

Closing the journal, I looked up to see fresh morning light pouring in through the kitchen window. A resolve swelled in my chest, and the verse that Mom had highlighted in my Bible before I had set off for college came to mind once again:

Trust in the LORD with all your heart
And do not lean on your own understanding.
In all your ways acknowledge Him,
And He will make your paths straight.

That morning, I was full of hope, but after yet another difficult day, evening still rolled around. I found myself once again back at my nightly ritual, and it didn't take long before the journal entry faded from my mind.

There would be two years of empty promises to come.

I had not yet hit rock bottom.

CHAPTER 19

MANAGEABLE

"I see new presents under the tree!" Callie squealed as she raced down the hallway looking for her shoes, with Wizard, our beloved greyhound, fast on her heels.

"I hope I got a Nintendo 64," Casen piped in. "My friends say they're awesome!"

"I want a mountain bike!" said Conner, putting his empty cereal bowl in the sink.

"Those sound like some pretty fancy toys," I said, sitting down with a fresh cup of coffee. "But I'll be sure to let Santa know what's on your list."

"Come on, Mom," Casen rolled his eyes in a way every fourteen-year-old has perfected. "Santa isn't real."

"What?" Callie emerged in the doorway. "Santa isn't real? But he eats the cookies we leave out every year." She looked at me, her expression a mix of hopeful expectancy and betrayal.

I shot Casen my best *now, are you happy?* look, suddenly grateful that Conner had stepped into the other room to get his shoes.

"Of course he's real, sweetie. Now everybody hurry up. You're going to be late for school. Casen, would you like me to drive you?"

"That's okay," he said, clearly feeling guilty. "I'll just take the bus." He grabbed his backpack, leaned over, and quickly kissed my cheek. "Sorry, Mom."

"It's all right, sweetie. You have a good day. I love you."

Casen's "I love you, too" was still hanging in the air when Callie and Conner emerged from the living room, shoes on and ready to go. I quickly gulped down what was left of my coffee, threw on a skirt and a top, and herded them both into the car. As we wound our way through the neighborhood to their elementary school, Conner counted the plastic reindeer in front yards while Callie hummed portions of *The Nutcracker Suite*, which she and her ballet class were performing selections from in a few days. After I dropped them off, I made my way back home, slowing the car a bit when I drove past the Harris Teeter.

I'm not going to stop . . . even though we only have one bottle left and I don't have to work today.

A blaring car horn brought me back to the road and the yellow light turning to red up ahead. Bewildered, I pressed on the brakes.

Marcy, it's not even 9 a.m. and you're already thinking about it . . .

Two years after the blackout—despite my promise to God— nothing had changed, with the exception of my ever-present desperation to quit drinking. Most mornings I'd swear off drinking, but by 5 p.m., a corkscrew was always close at hand. The apostle Paul's words had never rung so true: "I do not understand what I do. For what I want to do I do not do, but what I hate I do. . . . For I do not do the good I want to do, but the evil I do not want to do—this I keep on doing" (Romans 7:15, 19, NIV).

By now, my prayers sounded like a broken record:

Lord, I'm done with the drinking. I'm tired of feeling so . . . tired. So dependent on something other than you. Please give me strength to stop.

Lord, I overdid it again. I hate that I have this secret from Dev and the kids. What if they see something? Or pick up on how bad I feel in the mornings? I hate that I've become so good at hiding from them. From everyone. Please help me make the right choices today.

Lord, I'm scared by how much I've had to drink over the past week. I always thought I was a strong person, but right now I just feel so weak. Please help me. I've made a complete mess out of my life and I don't know how to get out of it.

The repetition of the prayers would be comical were the situation at hand not so dire—not only for myself, but for my family. To be sure, over the past seven years, I had managed never to drink and drive; I never drank more than a glass of wine in front of the kids; and I always pushed through the hangovers to attend every game, dance recital, and church gathering. I'd heard of such a thing as a "high-functioning alcoholic," and while "the *A* word" both repulsed and frightened me, if anyone fit that definition, it was me.

I arrived home to find Wizard waiting for me in the entryway.

I reached down and rubbed the back of his neck. "What am I going to do, Wiz?" He nuzzled the back of my knee with his nose. "Thank you, buddy," I said, scratching his ears. "That helps."

Suddenly, a novel idea popped into my head. *Maybe someone can help me beat this.*

I went into the kitchen and pulled the phone book down from the cabinet.

I wasn't even sure where to look. Under "S" for support group? Or maybe "T" for therapy? I opened the Yellow Pages to the front and started flipping through. Not two pages in, a small ad in bold lettering stopped me in my tracks:

Wondering if you are drinking too much?
Is alcohol taking a toll on your physical and mental
health?
Feel like you can't tell anyone?
There is help.

It didn't get much clearer than that.

In smaller text at the bottom of the ad was a list of locations and corresponding phone numbers. I scanned the list for the location farthest away. It was a church.

"Well, Wizard, if that isn't a sign, I don't know what is." I reached down and rubbed his ears. "I guess it couldn't hurt just to call. What do you think?" Wizard's tail wagged back and forth.

I dialed the number and a male voice picked up.

"Yes, I saw your ad, and I was . . ." Actually, I wasn't sure what I wanted. Fortunately, the man on the other end picked up on my hesitancy and jumped right in. Apparently, I was in luck. There was a group meeting that afternoon. He repeated the address and told me he hoped to see me there. I thanked him and hung up.

I left late that afternoon. It was the day Tinie came to help out, so I told her I had some errands to run and that Dev might be home before I got back. The kids all had after-school activities anyway, so odds were, nobody would even notice I was out.

As I glanced in the rearview mirror, the brim of one of Dev's old golf caps pulled down to the tip of my sunglasses, I was hoping nobody at this meeting would notice me either.

"I can't believe I'm even doing this." I sighed and shook my head. Actually . . . I could. Dad always said I was the kind of person who would jump out of an airplane first, *then* check to see if I had a parachute strapped to my back. Now that I thought about it, that's how I'd gotten myself into this mess in the first place—by rushing home from the hospital before I was ready and then keeping the extent of both my memory and my drinking problems a secret. In the process of convincing everyone—myself included—that I could handle it, I had effectively shut everyone else out—my parents, Dev, even God. The problem was, I couldn't handle it. Now I was hurtling toward the ground at breakneck speed, my entire support network completely oblivious to the fact that I was even falling.

I couldn't bear the thought of telling my friends and family that I was struggling. Maybe it would be easier in a room full of strangers.

⌒

The fellowship hall was in a building next to the church. A plain wooden cross hung on the wall, and on a folding table behind several rows of chairs was a stack of Styrofoam cups, a large silver coffee urn, and a plate of Oreos. I took a seat in the second row from the back. Sitting there under the fluorescent lights, with the afternoon sun pouring in, I felt oddly exposed. I pulled my cap down a little farther and looked around. I met a young woman's eyes several seats over, and she smiled at me. I smiled faintly and quickly looked down.

By the time the meeting started, almost every seat was taken. It was a really diverse group—men and women, some older, some my age, some younger. Most were dressed casually, in jeans and T-shirts, though one or two were wearing more formal business attire. I had to admit, they didn't look like I had expected a group of alcoholics to look. They looked . . . normal. They looked, well . . . like me.

A few more stragglers made their way in from the hallway and took their seats, and a middle-aged man stood up and called the meeting to order. "Any first-time visitors today?"

I saw a few hands go up in front of me. Eager not to draw any attention to myself, I opted to keep mine down.

"Well, we're glad all of you could make it. The upcoming holiday season can be difficult, what with all the parties, plus the added family and financial stress. But we will continue to meet every day through the end of the year—even on Christmas."

Why anyone would want to spend Christmas sitting in a fellowship hall eating Oreos and drinking weak coffee was beyond me. You'd have to be pretty desperate . . .

"So," he continued, "we'll start the same way we do every meeting: with a moment of silence, followed by the Serenity Prayer."

I looked around the room. If there was one skill I'd mastered over the past seven years, it was following other people's cues. Some were looking down, others had their eyes closed, and some just stared blankly ahead, sipping from their Styrofoam cups. I stared ahead until the group leader started reciting. When others joined in, I lowered my head.

God, grant me the serenity
to accept the things I cannot change,
courage to change the things I can,
and wisdom to know the difference.

I knew I had come across the prayer before, on a note card or bookmark, but it struck me anew read aloud in the fellowship hall.

I had asked God for healing countless times. I had never even thought to ask for acceptance. Or for peace in the waiting. I had always been too busy trying to heal myself. And then frustrated and angry when that healing didn't come.

"Next we're going to read through the twelve steps. They have been proven helpful for those who follow them in their entirety. If these are new for you, there are some free pamphlets on the table."

Curious as I was, there was no way I was getting up and walking over to that table. The leader began reciting the steps while the rest of us listened.

1. *We admitted we were powerless over alcohol—that our lives had become unmanageable.*
2. *We came to believe that a Power greater than ourselves could restore us to sanity. . . .*

The wording struck me as a little odd—almost cultish. I shifted uncomfortably in my chair. Maybe coming here was a mistake.

I looked at the clock and wondered how long I had to wait before I could leave without seeming rude.

Granted, some of what I was hearing sounded good enough, like step 5: *We admitted to God, to ourselves, and to another human being the exact nature of our wrongs.* God and I were well aware of how wrong my relationship with alcohol was. Nobody else was. Just the thought of admitting to anyone how much I was drinking reddened my cheeks. Still, two out of three wasn't bad.

Others, however, just struck me as . . . extreme, like *We made a list of all persons we had harmed and became willing to make amends to them all.* Had I really harmed anyone? Sure, I could have been more up-front and honest with Dev, but what I was doing wasn't *hurting* him in any way.

It was the first of the twelve steps, however, that struck me as most dire: *We admitted we were powerless over alcohol—that our lives had become unmanageable.*

Sure, there were times I went back for another drink when I shouldn't have, and yes, I often found myself looking ahead to that first welcome glass after dinner, sometimes before we had even cleared the breakfast dishes. But all things considered, would I really say my life was "unmanageable"? Given the circumstances, I thought I was managing my life pretty well. I'd raised three wonderful kids, I sang at church on Sundays, I ran my own consulting business, I had a lot of great friends and the love and support of my husband. That was hardly what I would call "unmanageable." I sat back in my chair defiantly.

After the facilitator finished reciting the twelve steps, he opened the floor for sharing. I slunk down a bit and was careful not to make eye contact with anyone. One by one, people told their stories. Some people shared how many years they had gone without alcohol, usually to a polite round of applause and choruses on congratulations. Others recounted times when their drinking had hurt their family or interfered with their jobs. One person remarked that they were starting the recovery process over again, having slipped and taken a drink at a Thanksgiving family gathering.

Lost jobs, broken families, not being able to handle a single drink at a holiday dinner . . . it was clear to me almost instantly. These people's lives were unmanageable. Mine was just fine. I felt better already.

After the facilitator made a few announcements and led the group in a closing prayer, I quietly stood up and slipped out the door, practically skipping on my way back to the car. If that was what it looked like to be an alcoholic, maybe I wasn't in as bad a shape as I feared.

On the way home, I passed a boutique wine shop that had opened a few months ago in a shopping center not far from our house. As if on autopilot, I pulled the car into the parking lot and browsed the aisles for several minutes before picking out a lovely bottle of chardonnay. After paying for my purchase, I settled back into the car, the bottle riding shotgun next to me.

Tonight, I thought, smiling to myself, *I am going to drink to celebrate the fact that I am not an alcoholic.*

CHAPTER 20

WHAT LIES AHEAD

DECEMBER 9, 1997

"Okay, everyone, whose turn is it to walk Wizard tonight?"

A chorus of "not me!'s" rang out from the kids, who were sitting with Dev in the den. I looked at Dev, who was settled in on the couch with Callie nestled next to him. He gave me a pleading smile before turning the channel to a rerun of *A Charlie Brown Christmas*.

"I guess I drew the short stick tonight," I sighed. "Come on, Wizard, let's go." He tilted his head and started wagging furiously, trailing close behind me while I went to the kitchen to grab a jacket and his leash.

The trees lining the quiet streets were lit up with twinkling lights. Usually the neighborhood was bustling with strollers and joggers and kids out riding their bikes until sunset. But tonight was silent save for a lone car passing by.

After a brisk walk up and down the street, Wizard and I slowly meandered our way up the driveway. I thought about yesterday's covert recovery meeting and the welcome realization that I didn't need help after all. I just needed to get serious. After all, I hadn't had a sip since I polished off that bottle of celebratory chardonnay last night.

This time I was really going to do it. I was going to stop. Starting tonight. I was going to go inside, brew myself a nice pot of tea, and spend the evening with my family.

No sooner did the resolve set in than a little voice inside countered with the rationalization . . . *Of course, since I'm not really an alcoholic, one more glass of wine won't matter one way or the other.*

Suddenly, the leash flew out of my hand. As if possessed, Wizard darted toward the bushes at the end of the driveway, his sight hound instinct to chase apparently rushing back after years of dormancy. As all eighty-five pounds of him lunged forward, my feet went out from under me, and I fell onto the driveway, my knees and hands stinging from the concrete upon impact.

"Wizard, what's wrong with you?!" I looked down at my hands to see scratches. He looked at me with his big doe eyes as if to say, "But there are baby bunnies back there, I just know it."

As I pushed myself up from the concrete, I glanced off to the left at the French doors leading into the den. It was almost pitch-black outside, but the room was bathed in a warm yellow light. Inside, a tableau worthy of Norman Rockwell came into focus.

Casen was lying on the couch next to Dev. I couldn't believe how tall he had become over the past year. He put his height to good use on the basketball court, and he had a competitive spirit I genuinely admired. My firstborn, who wanted to excel in all he attempted, was on his way to becoming a man.

Sitting next to Casen was Conner, who still sported the dimples that had turned my insides to butter since he was three. He constantly kept us in stitches with his jokes, but his gregariousness belied a sensitive spirit, which made him compassionate and hyperattuned to how the people around him were feeling.

Callie sat nestled under Dev's arm, captivated by whatever was on the TV. She still had the head full of curls she had worn since she was a baby. My sweet Callie was a bundle of energy—she'd never met a stranger and was always determined to keep up with her brothers.

And Dev. The man who had been my rock ever since I opened my eyes to a room full of strangers in the hospital seven years ago. Through all the years of trying to build a normal life, of physical weakness and mental fog, he had proven to be a best friend, a man of his word, and a brother in Christ who would intercede for me before God when I could no longer muster the words.

I drew in a sharp breath, overwhelmed by the beauty of the scene. This family. My family. The family I couldn't remember building, but that had nonetheless been stitched together through countless afternoons in the backyard and trips to the beach and too many game nights, car rides, and shared meals to count. It was the greatest gift I had been given. A gift that, until now, I had forgotten.

Staring through the French doors, I heard a voice speak from within me, strong and clear like the cool December breeze. It was a voice I knew and had longed to hear for so long, at once familiar and strange. It was so clear that it could have been audible, even though the night was as silent as a stone.

This is what I saved you for. The future, not the past.

As much as that father loves his children, I love you more.

And just as that father has his daughter in his arms, I am holding you, and I will never let you fall.

You just have to trust me.

As the tears fell down my cheeks, so did the walls I had erected around my heart when I told God that he could run the universe and I would handle my world. I was exhausted from holding up those walls. I was exhausted from trying to manage a world that had so obviously become unmanageable—just like the recovery group had said. I was exhausted from keeping layers of secrets from the people who loved me the most. I was exhausted from trying to save myself. It was suddenly clear what I needed to do.

I walked around the side of the house to our backyard, Wizard obediently trailing behind, the leash running on the ground next to him. I walked over to the small hill that rose near the back of the yard and knelt down. The grass under my jeans was wet and cold. I didn't care. I was finally ready.

Lord, I surrender the hope of recovering the memories I have lost. I see now that being fully present with my family and creating a future together is far more important than mourning the past. I also surrender the alcohol that has been keeping me from being fully present with them. And finally, I surrender control over my world, Lord. I want you to run my life. It is yours. It is all yours.

I opened my eyes and stood up. It felt as though a weight had been lifted from my shoulders, like a boulder had just rolled off them into the sea. I had made plenty of promises to God about the alcohol before in countless journal entries and remorseful morning prayers. But something about this time felt different. Solid. Secure. Because I wasn't just giving up the alcohol—I was giving up the control that the alcohol gave me the illusion of having. God was finally in control.

When I got back inside, Dev and the kids were still watching TV. Little did they know that in the time Charlie Brown had rescued his Christmas tree, my whole world had changed. I sat down on the couch next to Dev and nestled next to him, reaching over to hold Callie's hand. "You're back. That was quick," said Dev, leaning over to kiss me on the cheek.

Actually . . . it had taken seven years.

PART 4

THE PAINTING UNDER- NEATH

CHAPTER 21

SEEING WITH NEW EYES

"Tell me about the night you asked me to marry you," I said to Dev as we cuddled up on the back patio.

Two days after my first visit to the alcohol support group, I had returned to the meeting hall. This time I was serious. I was resolved. I was ready. I started my walk into sobriety on December 10, 1997, and alcohol would have no further place in my life.

Along with the removal of the alcohol came total honesty. This meant I had to be totally open with the people closest to me. Hiding things only cracked the door for more lies and more destructive behavior down the road. It was a little unnerving at first, especially when it came to admitting my dependence on alcohol to the kids. I was worried they might not understand—or worse—that they *would* and would think less of me as a result. But when the time came, they responded with a maturity well beyond their years, encircling me in a group hug.

When Conner asked if I would ever drink again, I explained that I would always be a pickle.

"What does *that* mean?" asked Callie, scrunching up her nose. She had never been a fan.

"Well . . ." I explained, "a pickle starts out as a cucumber. But once it's pickled, it can't go back to being a cucumber."

Casen nodded, but Conner and Callie exchanged confused looks.

"It just means that alcohol is bad for me," I said, "so I can't have it anymore."

"Ever?" Conner asked.

I shook my head. "Nope."

I also confessed to Dev the full extent of what I'd lost, though we decided not to delve into the lost memory issue with the kids right away for fear that it might upset them too much. True to form, he didn't see the lost memories as a shortcoming but rather as an opportunity to walk down memory lane. No matter what I asked, he was always happy to fill in the details.

"Well . . ." he started, his arms wrapped tightly around me, "we had just graduated from SMU, and I suggested that maybe we take a break from dating for a while."

"Was I upset?" I asked.

"Oh, no," he assured me. "We had been dating for over three years, and neither of us felt ready to get married yet, so we decided to just take a little time for ourselves. Anyway . . ." he continued, "after graduation, I went on a golf trip to Scotland with some of my fraternity brothers. Well, while I was there, I realized how much I missed you. So I sent you a telegram asking you to meet me for dinner as soon as I got back."

"Where did we go again?"

"The Enclave. You know . . . that fancy restaurant in north Dallas."

"Had you already bought the ring?" I asked, glancing down at the shimmering diamond on my finger.

"No," he chuckled. "I wasn't even planning to ask you that night. Honestly, I wasn't even sure what you'd say. I mean, we *were* supposed to be taking a break. But once we were there, you just looked so beautiful, I couldn't resist."

"Please tell me you at least got down on one knee," I said, cuddling into him further.

"You bet I did," he said proudly. "In fact, after I did it, all the waiters stopped what they were doing and applauded."

I looked up at him. "Did they really?"

"Yep," he said, smiling.

"And I'm assuming I said yes."

"Oh, you said yes, all right. In fact, before we left, you went into the ladies' room and told anyone who would listen that you had just gotten engaged!"

"I did not!" I looked at him, horrified.

"Oh, yes, you did! I was sitting there at the table, and one woman after another came out of the ladies' room smiling, laughing, and congratulating me. We had agreed to keep it quiet until you could tell your parents and your brother and sister, and you managed to keep it a secret for all of two minutes!"

I could barely contain my own laughter. "Yep, that sounds like me." It really did. In fact, hearing Dev tell it was almost as good as remembering it myself.

Dev had always been wonderfully supportive, but perhaps never more so than during those first few months of sobriety. That first Christmas, he helped me get through all the parties and gatherings we attended, getting me a Diet Coke before I could even make a choice, and pre-tasting various desserts for me to make sure they didn't have any alcohol in them (a sacrifice, to be sure).

When we went to the Cayman Islands the next year to celebrate Dev's fortieth birthday, I was worried that it would be hard to resist the fruity frozen drinks with tiny umbrellas perched on top. But once we got to the ocean, the sun, the sky, the water, *everything* seemed more colorful, more vibrant, and more alive than they had on previous vacations before I was sober, and I quickly realized I could live more fully without those fruity drinks.

In fact, everywhere I looked, colors seemed more vibrant. Even driving down the streets of Charlotte, I was amazed at how lush and green the grass and the trees were, the notable exception being the beautiful Bradford pear trees with their striking clusters of milky white blossoms that made the southern city look like a magical winter wonderland each spring. It was almost as though I was seeing colors for the first time. Food tasted better. I had more energy. Every hour of every day felt like a gift from God.

He had given me so much to be thankful for—family and friends who responded with compassion to my struggles with alcohol; Carolyn, a godly woman who guided me in my recovery; a healthy consulting business that gave me a sense of purpose as the kids got older and became more independent; a dear friend and second mother to my kids in Tinie, who took the boys and Callie to Hornets games and Panthers practices, to Renaissance Festivals and lunch dates. But most of all, he gave me the grace to let go of the past and to embrace each new day fully and completely—to let go of old, forgotten memories and focus instead on creating new ones that Dev, the kids, and I could all share together.

And the next fifteen years were full of memories. Like the time Conner broke his foot right before the start of football season his senior year of high school. He was crushed. It was all he could do not to cry when the doctor told him he wouldn't be able to play that season. But in true Conner fashion, he didn't let it get him down. In fact, he talked the coach into letting him serve as the assistant to the head coach. Oh, it ate him alive having to stand on the sideline every week. He so desperately wanted to play. So, when they got to the final game, he got permission to dress out—full pads and uniform.

Casen was away at college, but Dev, Callie, Tinie, and I were all there to cheer him on, whether he played or not. Midway through the fourth quarter, everyone in the stands started chanting, "Conner, Conner, we want Conner." There were only a few minutes left in the game, so the coach relented and sent Conner in, and he ended up making a great play. I will never forget the look on Conner's face when everyone came running up the field at the end to congratulate him. It was perfect in every way!

Or, the day Callie called us from Kenya where she was doing a mission trip with Young Life Africa. All we could hear was, "Mom, Dad, I need to talk to you," and then the phone would break up. Needless to say, Dev and I were panic-stricken. After all, Callie was only twenty and had never been out of the country before—at least without us. Finally, four connections later, she told us, "I'm going to stay in Africa a little longer, head to Tanzania, and climb Mount Kilimanjaro."

We said, "Are you crazy? You have no training. You don't have any cold weather gear. You cannot climb a mountain!"

But she just dug in her heels and said, "I'm gonna do it! And I'm gonna raise money for Young Life at the same time." And lo and behold, she climbed that mountain. One of her friends took a picture of her at the summit, and from that day forward, whenever I found myself worrying about Callie, I would just look at her smiling at the top of that mountain in a borrowed coat and climbing gear and laugh at myself for questioning her ability to do anything she set her mind to.

Or the day Casen was sworn in as an attorney. He looked so handsome in his best suit and tie. It was the most extraordinary experience. As he stood there before the judge taking his oath, all I could see was the little boy with a perpetual smudge on his cheek that I used to drop off at kindergarten. I didn't even attempt to hold the tears back that day. In fact, I don't know that I've ever been as proud as a parent as I was at that moment. I might have lost Casen's first six years, but *that* was a day I will *never* forget. Thirteen months later, Casen got a master of laws from Duke, another proud day for me.

Then there were our friends—we called them "Friends like Family"—six couples who walked with us through life. We traveled together, spent Christmas Eves together, held each other accountable in life. And although I had hidden it so well, when they found out about my drinking, they embraced and supported me completely.

As the years passed—all those years since God literally brought me to my knees in the backyard, I had been blessed more times and in more ways than I could count—through my daily interactions with the kids, watching them grow into caring, compassionate, accomplished adults; through a career I genuinely enjoyed; and through my ever-deepening relationship with Dev—God had proven faithful.

When my prayers for healing went unanswered, he was there. When I pushed him off to the side in favor of going it alone, he was always there. When alcohol took over my life, he was there. When I hit rock bottom, he was there. In a life forever scarred by the loss of memories, he had never forgotten me.

Just as David Chadwick had prayed over me in the ICU: "Because of the LORD's great love we are not consumed, for his compassions never fail. They are new every morning; great is your faithfulness" (Lamentations 3:22-23, NIV).

Each morning of my sobriety brought with it new beginnings, new blessings, and new hope. I used to dread the mornings—the searing headache, the confusion, the regret. But now . . . I couldn't wait to open my eyes and see what God had in store for me next.

CHAPTER 22

A PASSION RENEWED

"I think I want to start painting."

Dev stared at me across the kitchen table. He put down his newspaper, his eyebrows slightly raised. "Okay . . ." he said, hesitantly. "I did not see that coming."

"I know it sounds kind of out of the blue," I explained, "but a few weeks ago, I woke up with a burning desire to paint, and I haven't been able to stop thinking about it. Does that sound weird?"

Dev shook his head. "Not really. I mean you *did* major in studio art at SMU." He chuckled to himself. "Every time I saw you, you were covered in paint, charcoal, or clay. You absolutely loved it."

"Huh," I sat back in my chair. "Why did I give it up?" Strangely, there was very little to remind me of my former love for art around our home.

"Working full time and then having kids, Babe, didn't leave room for much else."

"I wish I could remember what I learned at SMU," I said. "I mean if I majored in it, I must have taken a lot of classes."

"You did," Dev said. "All of your textbooks are probably still in the attic."

I replayed that conversation with Dev in my head all morning. And that afternoon, I ventured back into the attic, sorting through stack after stack of boxes until I finally found what I was looking for—my old textbooks from SMU. Dev was right. From what I could tell, I had taken a whole complement of art history and studio art courses. Unfortunately, I couldn't remember any of it.

That night at dinner, I hit Dev with a little proposal of my own. "Dev, I think I'd like to step away from the consulting business and take some art classes."

Dev froze, his fork halfway to his mouth. "Are you serious?"

I nodded. "Yes. The boys are both out of the house, and Callie's busy with high school, her Young Life group, and friends. I feel like I need a fresh challenge."

"What about the consulting business?"

I shrugged. "I'll retire. I enjoyed it. I'd just like to do something more creative. And for whatever reason, God has really put this on my heart."

"He put it there ages ago." Dev laughed. "It just got buried under . . ."

"Marriage, kids, a coma, and wine?" I chuckled back.

He sat back in his chair, a smile tugging at the corners of his mouth. "Well . . . if that's what you want to do . . ."

I nodded.

Over the next several months I began to paint, taking some casual, introductory lessons. The tools seemed familiar to me—the texture of the paints and the feel of the palette knife with its wooden handle and its long, flattened edge. I chalked it up to muscle memory—my body remembering a skill that my mind could not, kind of like how I knew exactly how to hold, change, and feed Callie from day one.

But eventually I got frustrated, knowing I wanted more. I wanted to get serious, and I needed to find someone who could help me unlock my passion. I went to Dev one night and told him how I was feeling.

"Okay then," Dev said, always supportive. "Let's find you a person who can take you to the next level."

⁓

The studio was in an unassuming building fifteen minutes from the house. Arriving early for the first session, I waited in the car, flipping through the radio stations and watching the clock. As more cars pulled into the lot, my stomach churned. *What if this is a mistake? What if I'm not good enough to be here?*

There was only one way to find out.

I walked into the lobby, and instantly, I felt like I belonged. The walls were covered in large, inviting landscapes in the most brilliant colors—deep violets, lilacs, vibrant pinks, cadmium reds, cobalt teals, golden ochres, and brilliant greens—every inch of the paintings revealed a creative blend of colors that I would never have dreamed of putting together, yet somehow, they worked.

"Come on in!" a man's voice called out from inside the studio.

As soon as I entered the space, a whiff of turpentine and oil paint hit my nose. It was sharp and acidic . . . and familiar. It practically beckoned to me.

Oh, yes, I thought, taking it all in, *this feels right*.

The studio itself was a large warehouse with towering ceilings. At the end of the room a row of carts was parked next to a table filled with jars, brushes, and tubes of paint. In the middle of the room was a circle of easels, each adorned with a blank canvas.

Our group of a dozen or so walked over to a long table, where a bearded, bespectacled man wearing a black V-neck and khaki shorts flecked with paint was smiling and waving us in. I took one of the front seats and pulled out a notebook and pen, anxious to absorb everything I was about to learn. I had already lost the technical skills once; I wasn't going to lose them again.

"Welcome, everyone," he said. "My name is Andy Braitman. I'm excited you all are here. I'm not interested in you finishing paintings in this class; I'm interested in the process. In this space, you will create what only you can create—unique to you."

I could literally feel my heart rate increasing with excitement.

"We as artists must learn to nourish our roots. Let me say again, we are not here just to learn to paint, we are going to work on the roots—to understand what goes into creating. What others will see is our canopy that will be the result."

I had no idea what was down deep in me, but I couldn't wait to see what came forth.

Thank you, Lord. This is exactly what I needed.

For the next hour, Andy showed us how to create the underpainting. He made it look so easy, filling the canvas with broad brushstrokes that slowly began to tell a story. By the time he wrapped up, I was practically jumping out of my seat to get started.

"Okay," he said, "it's time to go and do. Choose the easel where you'd like to work, and get your paint. Don't worry about perfecting. Just get used to the feel of the palette knife and brush in your hand."

I followed the other students over to the selection of paints—a host of colors we could mix to create new colors. I chose cadmium red, ultramarine, burnt sienna, titanium white, and cadmium yellow. I carried my selections back to the circle of easels, chose one, and set my paints down.

"A blank canvas is so intimidating, isn't it?" whispered the young woman setting up at the easel next to mine. "It's hard to know where to even start."

I nodded quietly, but in truth, I was excited by the possibilities a blank canvas held. How could I not be? If the past seventeen years had taught me nothing else, it was that there are two ways to look at a blank canvas. You look at it as empty and become paralyzed by what's not there, or you can see it as a starting place to create something new and beautiful. And even if you make a mistake, it's never too late to start over. To change direction. To take what initially looked like a mess and transform it into something amazing.

"It's only intimidating if you leave it blank too long," I quipped, picking up a tube of burnt sienna.

I unscrewed the cap and squirted a couple of inches of paint onto the glass top of the small table next to the easel that I had just learned was called a *taboret*. Then I picked up the palette knife and slowly cut into the dollop of burnt sienna. I mixed the paint and began to wash the canvas in color. The warm tone would be a perfect underpainting.

"Nice job," came a voice from over my shoulder. Startled, I turned to the left and smiled at Andy.

"Thank you," I said. "I'm so excited to be here. So excited to be doing it again!"

"I can tell!" he said. "You seem very comfortable."

A smile crept across my face. "I am. I didn't think I would be. But now that I'm here, it feels so . . . right."

Andy watched me try different strokes on the canvas as I began to draw in the shapes from the reference photo I had chosen. I was excited for the opportunity to learn from Andy. His paintings spoke to me—images formed through a bold application of paint, creating beautiful texture. They were exciting displays on a canvas. Andy seemed to pour much of himself into his work—and I could tell he poured much of himself into his teaching as well. He was a talented teacher—patient and encouraging.

"So what made you decide to take up painting again?" he asked. I was grateful he hadn't asked why I had stopped. It's not that I was ashamed of my story—far from it. It just seemed like a lot to get into on my first day.

"I studied art in college," I told him. "But, then I had a family . . . things came up, and I ended up doing consulting work. Anyway, the kids are grown now, and a few months ago I woke up with a burning desire to paint."

He nodded. "Well, you've definitely come to the right place. Keep it up."

As he moved on to the next student, I stepped back from the easel to get a fuller view of what I'd done. I was excited over the work in progress. I had chosen a photo of a barn with a rusty orange roof in the middle of a lush field. Barns were a common subject for beginner oil paintings, but I was also drawn to the barn because of a childhood spent in Texas, where barns were a dime a dozen. Mom and Dad used to have one of my grandmother Lois's barn paintings hanging in our kitchen, and I couldn't help thinking of her as I added tufts of moss green around the barn's edges. I might have lost thirteen years from the middle of my life, but the sights, sounds, and smells of the Texas farmland I grew up in were as deeply ingrained as the feel of the palette knife in my hand.

Over the next several months, I soaked up Andy's teaching like a sponge. He had a mastery over color like no one I had ever seen. He taught us about color, line, and composition and how to add layers and clean our brushes. The pungent smell of turpentine never got old. Every Tuesday when I woke up, I couldn't wait to get to the studio. And that night, I'd bring home some of my paintings and set them up around the house, which was starting to feel like a gallery. But now, as the class was coming to an end, I wasn't sure what to do with these skills. And I was worried that if I didn't keep painting, they'd be lost, just as they had been before.

I was putting the finishing touches on my final piece when Andy came up behind me and said, "Marcy, can I speak with you after class?"

"Of course." I tried to sound casual, but honestly, was it ever a good sign when a teacher asked to see you after class? For the rest of the class, my mind raced with questions. Had I done something wrong? Did he not like my final piece? Did I not do as well as he had hoped?

When the class ended, Andy addressed the whole group. "You've all been wonderful. Keep practicing, keep learning, and if you're interested in going further, there's a sign-up sheet for the summer workshops and fall classes out at the reception desk."

As the group slowly dispersed, I mingled with some of the other students in the lobby, admiring their finished landscapes and still lifes, trying to ignore the nervous lump growing in the pit of my stomach. Finally, I made my way to the back of the studio, where Andy was standing in front of an easel, paintbrush in hand, ready to make his mark on a fresh canvas.

"You wanted to speak to me?"

"Yes, Marcy." He set his brush down. "How did you feel about your first session?"

"I enjoyed every minute of it! Honestly, the only thing I want to do right now is paint."

"That's what I wanted to talk to you about." He paused just long enough for my mind to start racing again. "I have an artist-in-residence program starting in the fall. I want you and Allison to participate. It's six months, and you'd be here every weekday from 9 a.m. to 4 p.m., taking more classes. We'll be getting into some more advanced subjects, and I think it'd be a great opportunity for you."

My mouth dropped halfway to my chest. "Wow . . . Thank you, Andy. I'm honored by the invitation." *Careful . . . don't get ahead of yourself.* "I'd like to talk to my husband before I commit to anything, but please know that I'm definitely interested."

"Great!" he said. "Just let me know what you decide."

I thanked him again, then practically skipped to my car. When Dev got home later that day, I ran out to meet him.

"So . . . how was the final class?"

"Well," I broke into a grin, "it might not be my final class. Andy invited me to join his artist-in-residence program!"

"Marcy, that's wonderful!" Dev beamed and pulled me into a hug. "Talk about a vote of confidence. How long is the program?"

"Six months," I said, "seven hours every day. It's a pretty big commitment," I hedged, "but I have the time now that the kids are gone and I'm not working."

"I think it's great," Dev assured me. "Go for it!"

For the next several months, I woke up with painting on the brain. After devotions, coffee, and a brisk walk with Annie and Buddy, our little mixed-breed dogs, I'd drive over to the studio, put on an apron, and start painting. It usually wasn't long before I'd fall into a rhythm—a cut of the knife here, a stroke of the brush there—there was a flow to it. Sometimes I had an image or color scheme in mind; other times, I came in blind and simply went where the paint led me. Yellow ochre and burnt orange kept cropping up in unlikely places, for no other reason than that they made me happy.

As Andy introduced more advanced subjects, pushing me beyond my typical barns, cows, and expansive Texas fields, I approached each one—be it an abstract or a live model—as a new, exciting challenge. The warm and welcoming environment of the studio where everyone was learning together helped calm the perfectionist tendencies that had led me to fake being fine in the previous chapters of my life. Here, there was no way to fake it. Either you were growing in your abilities, or you weren't. Mistakes were welcome because they meant you were pushing yourself out of your comfort zone. And I was feeling more comfortable every day.

Finally, after years of feeling as though everything had been taken away from me, I had gotten something back.

CHAPTER 23

WORLDS OF COLOR

MARCH 2011

It was Monday morning around six thirty, one week before my graduation from the artist-in-residence program. I got dressed for the day, eager to head back to the studio to finish my final painting of the residency, a vase containing large, cheery sunflowers against a cerulean blue background. I put on a knit top and paint-speckled jeans, grabbed my new laptop, and headed downstairs. The next thing I knew, my feet came out from under me and I was hurtling down the stairs headfirst. When I finally landed at the bottom, my knees hit the floor, absorbing the entire impact, and my left knee made a strange, airy sound like a dog toy. A few seconds passed before the screaming pain lit up my entire left leg. I looked down, half expecting it to be detached from my body. When I tried to move my leg, it wouldn't budge, and a searing pain pulsed my kneecap. Already I could feel it starting to swell beneath my jeans.

"DEV! DEV!"

Dev came running out of his office, a panicked look on his face. "What is it?! What happened?"

I tried to move my leg again. It was twisted outward unnaturally, but when I went to adjust it, every millimeter of movement sent pain radiating throughout my body.

"My leg! I just fell down the stairs! There's something wrong with it!"

Dev rushed to my side and reached down to adjust it.

"No! Don't move it!"

"Okay, okay . . ." He took his hands away. "Let me call Jerry," Dev said after a few panicky seconds.

Dev ran back to the office to call Jerry Barron, our orthopedic surgeon friend, as I tried to focus on my breathing. The pain kept crashing like waves against my body, unrelenting. I could hear the urgency in Dev's voice from the other room.

"Jerry's going to meet us over at his office," Dev said, maneuvering around me. "He said to have you put your arms around my neck, and I'm going to hold you with your legs dangling loose. He said that's the easiest way to get you to the car without injuring your knee even more."

I looped my arms around Dev's neck, and he slowly lifted my body up alongside his. He tried to let my legs dangle, but it was impossible to keep them completely straight. Any slight bend in my leg sent spasms of pain through my body. Not wanting to scream in poor Dev's ear, I kept my eyes closed and focused on my breathing.

The fifteen-minute drive across town to Jerry's office felt like hours. I lay stretched out sideways in the back seat, trying to keep my leg straight, bracing at each stoplight and bump in the road. As anxious as I was to get some relief from the pain, I dreaded finding out the extent of what I had done. After all, I hadn't had the best of luck in hospitals.

When Dev finally pulled the car up to the entrance, Jerry was waiting there for us in a T-shirt and jeans. Dev carefully helped me out of the back seat and into a wheelchair.

"I'm pretty sure I know what happened, based on what you described," Jerry said. "We'll have to do X-rays to be sure, but my guess is you shattered your kneecap. And the fact that you can't bend your leg means the tendon's probably torn as well."

There were no two ways about it. That sounded bad.

The nurse wheeled me into the X-ray room toward a long metal table, the ever-present stench of ammonia trailing around me. By this point, my heart rate had increased, and I felt clammy all over. I would never get used to the sights, sounds, and smells of a hospital.

Dev and Jerry stayed out in the hallway while a nurse and a technician got me situated on the long table. I closed my eyes and tried to focus on happy times, thinking back to our family trip to Aruba with the kids as they maneuvered the machine around my left knee, a *whirr* and a *click* accompanying each image.

"Hang in there, Marcy," the tech said, "we're almost done."

Please, God . . . please let it not be bad . . .

Several minutes later, as everyone hovered around the monitor behind the protective glass, I overheard the technician utter the word *catastrophic*, and my heart sank.

Why is this happening, Lord? What about the artist-in-residence program? How will I ever be able to finish if I can't even stand up?

———

Several nights later, I lay awake at home next to Dev, fighting the pain that enveloped my left knee and leg. It was an unwelcome guest that made the night seem to stretch on and on.

Jerry had repaired my kneecap and reattached my torn tendon, but the long road to recovery ahead called into question why God would have let me fall back in love with painting only to take it away from me—even if only for a little while. Aside from Dev and the kids, it was the thing that brought me the most joy, and the thought of not being able to go into the studio every day and do what I loved was almost more than I could bear.

Maybe it was a sign that painting had become too important—that it was too consuming, too central to my sense of self-worth. Maybe it was God's way of making sure I was trusting him instead of trying to go it alone, as I had done so many times before. I had to confess I had no idea what he was up to. I just knew that Scripture commanded me to be still and know that he is God (see Psalm 46:10). Now, with the doctors predicting that I had months of physical therapy ahead of me, I had no choice.

Be still & know that I am God

Whatever God was doing, I really needed him to show up because the pain felt unbearable—especially without pain meds to help. At our recovery meetings, friends had warned how easy it was for one addiction to morph into another. So when the doctors handed Dev a prescription for powerful pain medicine, I only took a few, then stopped for fear of getting hooked. I had gone more than thirteen years without alcohol. Now was not the time to stand atop a slippery slope. It would be far too easy to fall.

So instead, I lay there silently, trying to keep my left leg perfectly straight, grimacing from the pain and the discomfort of desperately needing to use the restroom. I couldn't get out of the bed on my own, but I also couldn't bear to wake Dev up again. If I was going to be dependent on him for everything for the next several weeks, he was going to need a decent night's sleep.

Lord, the pain is so intense . . . I don't know how I'm going to get through this night.

I lay there in silence, waiting for God to show up, but the only presence in the room was the pain.

An angel in the corner would be great right about now. Or an audible voice. Maybe a burning bush? Something, God. I need to know you're with me.

I glanced over to the corner. Nothing there but a dresser.

I need your strength to get through this . . . please.

Just then, a familiar verse flashed through my mind: "I can do all things through Him who strengthens me."

Philippians 4:13. It was the verse Dad helped me to remember when things were hard growing up. The verse I had shared with Casen, Conner, and Callie before all their school assignments, tests, big games, and as they were leaving the nest and making their way out into the world. It was such a well-known verse, and it held a special resonance for me. Granted, tonight I was hoping to hear something new from God. Yet Philippians 4:13 kept flashing in my mind like a neon sign.

"I can do all things through Him who strengthens me."

Is that all you have for me, Lord?

"I can do all things through Him who strengthens me. I can do all things through Him . . . I can do . . ."

I repeated the verse in my mind until finally, somehow, I fell asleep.

The next morning I awoke feeling exhausted. Dev was breathing softly next to me. *Poor guy; I can't wake him up just yet.* I reached over to the devotional on my bedside table, *Jesus Calling*, by Sarah Young. I turned to the entry for that day and my jaw dropped. Right there was, of all things, the Amplified version of Philippians 4:13:

> I have strength for all things in Christ Who empowers me [I am ready for anything and equal to anything through Him Who infuses inner strength into me; I am self-sufficient in Christ's sufficiency].

This was his confirmation, however quiet and understated, that he had heard my prayers that night and was inviting me to rest in his strength rather than my own.

I kept reading Young's entry for the day:

It is good that you recognize your weakness. That keeps
you looking to Me, your Strength. Abundant life is not
necessarily health and wealth; it is living in continual
dependence on Me. Instead of trying to fit this day into
a preconceived mold, relax and be on the lookout for
what I am doing. This mind-set will free you to enjoy Me
and to find what I have planned for you to do. This is far
better than trying to make things go according to your
own plan.

The words were a balm. Even though I had no idea what God's
plan was for the artist-in-residence program, whether he had willed
the injury or merely allowed it to happen, it was clear he had taken
me to a place of vulnerability—a place where I had to depend on
him.

I kept reading:

Don't take yourself so seriously. Lighten up and laugh with
Me. You have Me on your side, so what are you worried
about? I can equip you to do absolutely anything, as long as
it is My will. The more difficult your day, the more I yearn
to help you. Anxiety wraps you up in yourself, trapping you
in your own thoughts. When you look to Me and whisper
My Name, you break free and receive My help. Focus on
Me, and you will find Peace in My Presence.

Thinking ahead to this new day and all the long days that would
follow, I took these words to heart.

Jesus, I prayed, *I need your help to get through this day. And the next.
Through it all, help me to find peace in your will.*

In the first weeks of recovery, God made sure I didn't take myself so seriously. After all, it's hard to be prideful when you have to rely on other people for everything, from getting dressed to going to the bathroom. Dev, of course, stepped up as he had so many times before. There was no hiding from him how weak and vulnerable I was, yet he met it all with cheerfulness and grace.

My girlfriends stepped up as well. They knew how much pain I was in and that I needed companions to walk alongside me as I recovered. They took turns dropping off meals, taking me to and from physical therapy, walking the dogs, and sitting with me to distract from the boredom. A few times, when I'd hear the back door open, I'd yell out, "I have to go to the bathroom, so whoever you are—I need your help!" If nothing else, it was a wonderful lesson in humility.

As the days in bed dragged on, my leg still felt sore, but my mind was getting antsy, so Dev set me up in bed with a piece of glass, a few tubes of paint, a palette knife, and a stack of magazines so I could practice mixing my paints to match the pictures in the magazines. Page after page, I would work until the colors were spot-on. I wanted to master this skill—to see a color and know how to get it by mixing other colors together. I might not have had the strength to stand at an easel, but that didn't mean I couldn't keep honing the skills. At some point, I would get back into that studio, and when I did, I wanted to have made at least *some* progress.

There were moments when the pain would bowl me over and leave me utterly depleted. As a distraction, I would journal:

Monday

What a week it has been. As I got home, I began to ask the question, "Why, God? . . . Why am I in this place?" Have I made my art too important? Lord, I don't know what you have planned for me, but I want to hear from you. I want to learn in this place. I do believe that you have a plan and a purpose for every minute I am in this bed. Will you bless me as I seek you?

And I kept painting.

Some days were heavy with discouragement. Painting exercises using the magazines was nothing like being in the studio. I wanted the freedom to stand in front of a pure, new canvas and watch my creation come to life. I had learned in the residency that I had to wait for a layer of paint to dry before pushing ahead to the next detail. That was the hardest part, in the studio as in recovery: I couldn't rush the process. The waiting was harder than the pain or the boredom. I took my frustrations to God:

Wednesday

I find myself very discouraged this afternoon. I want to be up on my feet. I want to go back to the studio and paint. I want to be self-sufficient again . . . not totally dependent on others for everything. Why, Lord, has this happened? What am I to learn during this time of waiting? This is so slow . . . so quiet . . . so lonely. How do I do this? Just as I asked these questions, I received this encouraging email from Jane. It reminded me that I must stay focused on you, Lord . . . I must listen . . . I must seek your face . . . with a thankful heart.

Do not get discouraged—just let God grab your right hand and pull you up/lift you up (Isaiah 41:10). Rest in him/praise him for the stillness. It's these moments of weakness that he uses for his glory. Listen to him b/c I'm guessing he has some things to tell you.

Jane

Over those weeks, immobile and sore and frustrated and not able to do all the things that I loved, a funny thing happened: I spoke to God, and he spoke back. The more I turned to him with the full range of my experiences, the more he spoke to me through his Word and through the encouragement of family and friends.

Monday

*The days are passing . . . so slowly. I have learned just how
helpless I am. Lord, you have been so faithful. When I ask for
the small things from this bed, you provide. I see your hand
in my day . . . over and over. People come when I need them.
They bring food . . . they fix my plate and serve me. Today
I was so lonely . . . I needed people . . . I needed help with
Buddy and Annie. They needed to go for a bathroom walk . . .
I asked you, Lord . . . crazy? It seemed easier than calling on
people. I have had to ask so many people for so many things.
I hate being so needy. I had barely finished praying when my
neighbor Melissa showed up with a beautiful dinner for tonight
and also offered to walk Buddy and Annie. I was speechless!
Then later this afternoon, Jeanie, Kim, Betsy, and Ann came
and sat with me. They made me laugh . . . They loved me well.
You have provided exactly what I have needed. Thank you.*

For the second time in my life, God had literally brought me to my knees to teach me that without Christ, I was weak, but with Christ, I was strong.

And something else was happening in that time of waiting. Before my injury, I saw colors in broad categories: red was red, blue was blue, green was green. But as I mixed colors, day by day, I began to see how a green could be vibrant or grayed, deep or pale. I grew to love the range of blues I could create, and felt my heart drawn to subtle shades I hadn't realized could exist before. Even as I waited for my body to heal, my color mixing muscles were stretched and strengthened, and I felt whole worlds of color opening up in front of me.

CHAPTER 24

SPACE TO GROW

"I'm ready to go back to the studio."

Dev had just finished dressing me for the day and was getting ready to go to work. He stood at the foot of the bed, eyeing my left leg. It was stretched out on top of the sheets, and the long, garish incision from surgery was still raised and red across my kneecap.

"Are you sure you're feeling up to that?" he asked hesitantly. "I know you're going stir-crazy being stuck here, but . . ."

"Out of my mind," I corrected him.

"I just don't want you to push yourself too hard and mess up your knee."

"I know . . . I don't either," I said, noting his furrowed brow. "But the physical therapist said I'm doing well for only a month in. The color mixing exercises have helped, but I don't want to lose everything else I learned from Andy."

"I know you don't, babe." He paused a moment. "Did you want to head over today?"

"I'd like to try."

"Okay," he said, forcing a smile, "let me get the wheelchair in the car."

Poor guy. I knew he was worried, but every day I went without painting—real painting—was just torture. Even if I couldn't stand up, if I could get back to the studio, at least I would have access to all the proper tools. And if I could just smell the linseed oil again . . .

An hour later, after a comic display of contortions, maneuvering the stairs, and getting me into the back seat of the car, we were finally on our way. It was a sunny spring morning, and the tulips and daffodils were beginning to pop up in our neighbors' yards. It all seemed to reflect my excitement at finally getting to head back to the studio.

The parking lot was nearly full. Dev lifted me into the wheelchair, being careful to keep my leg straight at all times. As we rolled down the hallway toward the studio, the scent of turpentine washed over me, and instantly, I was in heaven.

"Marcy!" Andy practically did a double take before setting his brush down and coming to the door to meet us. "Well, hi! What a surprise! How are you feeling?"

"I'm okay," I assured him. "I've been getting a lot of help from Dev and friends. And," I smiled brightly, "I've been trying to paint."

"Is that so?" He looked down at my leg quizzically.

"Yes. I have a little oil paint set at home, and I've been practicing mixing colors to match the photos in magazines."

His eyebrows arched in surprise. "Really?"

"Of course, it's nothing like being here," I quickly acquiesced.

"Well," he said, smiling, "you're welcome back whenever you feel ready."

"Oh, I'm ready."

"Well, okay," he said, chuckling. "Let's get you set up, then."

Dev wheeled me over to the circle of easels in the middle of the room while Andy worked to adjust an easel down to eye level. Then he brought over the sunflower painting I had been working on and helped me set up my paints. It took some time to get used to painting from the wheelchair, but once I got started, I completely forgot I was sitting. By the time I had cleaned up and Dev had arrived to drive me home, the sun was beginning to dip below the horizon. It was the best day I had had in a month.

⁓

Recovery stretched on like a marathon. About two months in, I was alternating between resting in bed and having friends load the wheelchair into the car and drive me to the studio. Finally, the day came that I had been dreading for weeks. The bones and tendon had healed, but that scar tissue had built up around my knee, so they were going to have to bend it to break it up and start restoring my mobility. And based on everything I had heard, it was not going to be pleasant. The morning of the appointment, I took ibuprofen, but as soon as I got onto the table, the physical therapist handed me a towel.

"What's this for?" I asked.

"To bite down on if you need to," he said. I gulped as he placed his hands on my left leg.

Oh, Lord . . . please get me through this.

Just then, a tall, willowy woman I had never seen before walked into the room and climbed onto the exercise bike next to the table. I watched as she began pedaling.

"Okay, ready, Marcy?" said the therapist, paying no mind to the woman.

I nodded and held the towel to my mouth, but I was transfixed by this strange woman in the room with us. Just as the therapist started to bend my knee, the woman looked at me and said, "I can do all things through Him who strengthens me!"

That's my verse!

When I looked down, my knee was already bent. I yelped quietly into the towel as pain shot through my leg, but I was in so much shock it hardly registered. When I looked up again, the woman was gone.

"Who was that?" I asked the therapist.

"Who was who?" he asked quizzically.

"That woman. The one on the exercise bike."

He looked over at the empty bike, then at me.

"What woman?" the therapist asked. "There was nobody else here just now except us."

"But . . ." I looked over at the bike, trying to remember the position the pedals had been in when I arrived.

As the physical therapist's assistant brought ice for my leg, I continued to stare at the bike. Before I knew it, a chuckle escaped my lips.

You're so good to me, God. You even care about my physical therapy.

—

After that appointment, I was much more mobile, even though I had to use a walker, then crutches. Back at the studio, my old artist-in-residence partner, Allison, and other students helped me set up at an easel, where I now sat perched on a stool, working on small paintings of barns, landscapes, and flowers. The setup was a bit awkward, but the joy that I found being immersed in painting again was worth it.

"If you ever need help getting to the bathroom, just let me know," came a voice from behind me. I turned slightly to find a woman with dark, shoulder-length hair and a bright smile standing just off to my right.

"Oh my gosh, that's so sweet of you," I said. "I might just take you up on that!"

We quickly struck up a conversation, and her outgoing spirit drew me to her like a moth to a flame. Her name was Adrian Chu Redmond, and she had recently begun taking lessons as a birthday gift from her husband. Like me, she worked a lot in landscapes, using bold brushstrokes and vivid hues, signing her works in bright red symbols as a nod to her Chinese heritage. She typically came in on Thursdays, and whenever she was there, we would talk. One Thursday, as we were standing side by side at the sink cleaning our brushes, she asked, "So have you had any training in art before now?"

I paused.

Might as well tell her the truth.

"Sort of," I began. "I studied studio art in college, but I really don't remember any of it because I was in a coma."

Adrian laughed. "I totally understand. I feel like I'm in a coma all the time!"

Let me try that again . . .

I chuckled, not wanting her to feel bad for misunderstanding. "No, I'm serious—I was in a coma—back in 1990. When I came out of it, I couldn't remember anything that had happened over the past thirteen years."

Adrian looked up and stared, studying my face. When she saw that I was serious, she inhaled sharply. "Oh my gosh . . . that's like . . . movie-story dramatic."

"It's a long story," I said, smiling. "But I'm doing a lot better now. I've had a lot of help and support from family and friends over the years. And of course, my faith has kept me grounded."

"That's incredible," she said, shaking her head in disbelief. "I'd love to hear more sometime . . . maybe over drinks."

I chuckled to myself. The poor thing was already reeling enough. That part of the story could wait for another day.

"What about you?" I asked, changing the subject. "Have you taken lessons before?"

She shrugged. "My mom is an artist, and we always did lots of art projects while I was growing up, but I haven't had any formal training until now."

"It sounds like we're on parallel tracks then," I said, smiling.

We continued to rinse out our brushes for a few more minutes, then she turned to me and said, "I don't know where you paint or what your setup is—and feel free to say no if the timing isn't right— but have you ever thought about renting a studio?"

I put my brushes down.

"It's so funny you say that," I said. "My husband and I were just talking this week about how crowded the house is getting. I just don't know where else to put the paintings."

"Our house is crowded too," she said. "I've been thinking about renting a space of my own once classes are over. Let me know if you'd ever want to go look at spaces. I have a lead on a place in NoDa."

NoDa, short for North Davidson, was an artsy neighborhood on the northeast side of town, with lots of boutique shops, brunch spots, and a couple of eclectic museums. It was a bit far from home, but whenever Dev and I had visited, I always enjoyed seeing the public murals and sculptures lining the sidewalks.

"Wow, that sounds like it could be great. Can I get back to you on that?"

"Of course!" she said. "I know we're just getting to know each other, but I think it'd be fun to rent together."

That night, I recounted the conversation to Dev. He looked at the newest stack of paintings near the staircase, smiling. "It probably *is* time to think about that." Then he gave me a hug and said, "Whatever you want to do . . . we'll make it work."

The next morning, I wrote in my journal.

Lord, thank you for restoring the painting back to me . . . for allowing me to paint while I'm still recovering. For teaching me to rely on you rather than myself for daily strength. I don't believe you were punishing me with the fall . . . maybe just inviting me to learn about how trustworthy you are.

*Lord, I have a big decision to make . . . whether to take a
leap and move into a studio. I don't know how the financials
will work out. Where all of this painting is going. But I believe
you've led me to Adrian for a reason. She already feels like a fast
friend, someone I could work alongside and encourage. Please let
me know whether I'm on the right path.*

～

Several months later, after the walker and crutches were gone and I
could drive on my own, I headed out to the studio space Adrian and
I had rented in NoDa. It was small, with a concrete floor, gas heating, and exposed metal pipes on the ceiling, but it provided enough
room for both of us to store our canvases and supplies and to work
next to each other without getting in each other's way. When we
first walked in with the landlord, something about the space, with
its natural light and shabby chic charm, just felt right, so we signed
the lease and began setting up shop.

As I had expected, Adrian and I became really good friends upon
arriving at the NoDa studio, painting next to each other, all the while
chatting like sisters. We quickly learned of some uncanny similarities:
we both had three children, two boys and a girl. We both had a son
named Conner. Adrian's other son was named Devin—whom they
called Dev—and her daughter's name was Ally. We had both faced
a couple of similar medical issues over the years. And, most important, we both wanted to be the best artists we could be without ever
competing or sharing a cross word. Our friendship was such a clear
gift from God.

Today, however, I had the studio to myself, and I was grateful for
the quiet. As much as I loved chatting with Adrian, this morning I
just wanted to be alone with my work . . . and with God.

The last several months had been so emotionally draining—losing
my only creative outlet, wondering if I would ever be able to get

back in the studio again, and worrying that I might lose all the new skills Andy had taught me. Now that things were back to normal, I just wanted to spend some time in quiet worship, celebrating all the miraculous twists and turns that had brought me to this point—from the coma and my struggles with alcohol to my recovery and the restoration of my love of painting—somehow, despite the setbacks, the disappointments, and the mess I made of things, year after year, layer upon layer, God had created a masterpiece.

Overcome, I looked down at my feet and smiled as a lone tear splashed to the floor. Somehow it seemed appropriate. I was, after all, standing on hallowed ground.

CHAPTER 25

LAYERS OF MEANING

"Marcy, it's me." Mom's voice sounded strained in her voicemail, as though she'd been crying. "Your dad has taken a turn for the worse. I need you to come home as soon as possible."

My legs went out from under me, and I slumped down on the edge of the bed.

"What's going on, sweetheart?" Dev asked, loosening his tie.

We were in New York attending an art show at a swanky Manhattan gallery that was featuring some of Adrian's work. It had been an amazing year. In addition to Adrian's show, some of my own work had been picked up by a small gallery in Charlotte and a larger one in Atlanta. We had even made some individual sales. To my surprise and delight, what had started out as a hobby for both of us had blossomed into a very successful business. Things had never been better. Then . . .

"It's Dad," I said, looking down at the phone. "Mom says I need to get back to Beaumont right away. She says he's not going to be here much longer."

We had known about Dad's diagnosis for a while. Shortly before Casen graduated from college, Mom and Dad had told me while I was visiting in Texas that he had Parkinson's disease. They had gone to the doctor for a series of tests after Dad began to think something was wrong. He always was the best diagnostician. Of course, Mom and Dad being Mom and Dad, they totally downplayed it.

"I feel just fine," Dad had assured us.

"Are you sure?" I had asked. "It sounds serious."

But Mom just waved off our concerns and said, "Don't you worry. Your dad's going to be around for a long, long time."

Later that night, I pulled Dad aside and asked him if he and Mom were being totally honest with us. He looked at me, that telltale sparkle in his eye, and said, "Everything's going to be okay."

And for the longest time, everything was. I would fly down to Texas every three or four months to visit, just as I always had. And of course, we continued to get together for the holidays. It wasn't until Callie was in college that I started to really notice Dad slowing down. And there was something different about his smile. At that point, I started to realize that our time together might be limited, so my trips down to Beaumont became even more precious to me.

On my most recent visit, Dad hadn't been able to move or speak much. Mom, Ann, and I took turns sitting with him, reminiscing about our childhoods, family beach trips, golf games, all his accomplishments as an air force captain and later as a dentist, and how much his grandkids loved and missed him. I told him about my painting, that galleries were starting to take an interest, and that I had even sold a couple of pieces. He wasn't able to say much, but the sparkle in his eye told me he was proud. And now . . .

"Oh, Marcy," Dev sat down beside me and put his arm around

my shoulders. For the first time in my life, I was too shaken to even cry.

"What do you want to do?" Dev asked. "Should we try to get you a flight directly to Houston?"

As the logistics of how to get to Beaumont as quickly as possible began to swirl in my mind, I couldn't shake the last image I had of Dad, sitting in a chair under a blanket. I wished I could magically transport myself to his side, so I could hold his hand and tell him everything was going to be okay.

"I need to go back to Charlotte first," I finally said to Dev, who had already started researching flights on his laptop. "I need to get clothes for the funeral." I pinched the bridge of my nose, hot tears forming behind my eyes. "How am I going to tell the kids?"

By early afternoon the next day, Dev and I were back home. I had started to pack my suitcase, but I couldn't bring myself to put the black dress hanging near the back of my closet in it just yet. The dress just hung there staring at me, reminding me of what I wasn't ready to face.

I couldn't imagine a world without my dad. His was the first face I had seen when I awoke from my coma. He was the one who always assured me that no matter how painful or difficult life got, everything was going to be okay. Many of the memories I had from before the coma involved my dad. The infectiousness of his laugh. The way he would lead Christmas carols as we gathered together on Christmas Eve, and our famous father/daughter shopping trips, and how he would always wait in the driveway for me to come home from school, an enormous smile on his face.

Someone once told me that having a wonderful father here on earth is like getting a taste of what it will be like to spend eternity with our heavenly Father someday. It's the same image, really—a loving, caring father standing there, waiting for you to come home, an enormous smile on his face because he loves you so much he can't wait to see you.

The black dress could wait. Right now, more than anything, I just wanted to paint.

I grabbed my purse and headed out to Adrian's and my new studio. Our old space in NoDa had served us well for two years, but when our lease was up, we decided to move to a studio closer to our homes.

I was working bigger now. Gone were my days of painting on compact, 11 x 14 canvases. I realized I didn't enjoy painting all those small details. Painting everything so tiny just gave me ants in my ears. I wanted to go big. Now, my paintings measured 40 x 40, 48 x 48, sometimes even 60 x 60. I liked canvases that were big enough to feel as though I could step into them, like a portal into another world, and if ever there was a time I needed to step out of this world and into another, it was now.

Lately, my paintings had definitely become more otherworldly. Several months ago, I was standing in front of a painting of another barn, and a daring thought came over me: *I don't want to play by the rules anymore. I'm going to make this barn wonky and see what happens.* So I started to focus on the colors and lines and shapes—the building blocks of artistic form—rather than the content. The barn ended up purple and green, and the gallery in Charlotte wanted it immediately. So, I began abstracting other things like fields, flowers, and night skies. The color and the lines just spoke to me, and the abstract form felt natural and right. I had finally found my true artistic vision, and it was positively energizing.

But today, by the time I had arrived at the studio, set up a large canvas, and mixed a load of paint, I was spent. My thoughts were consumed with Dad. I had known for months that the end was imminent. Parkinson's was a degenerative disease without a cure, and at age seventy-nine, we all knew that even Dad could hold on for only so long. But up until now, I had managed to keep the grief at bay.

As the salty tears began cascading down my cheeks, I stared at the blank canvas, unable to lift the brush and with no idea how to fill the empty space.

Finally, I took a long, thin brush and dipped it in a deep, rich, red paint. In large scripted letters, I painted the only thing I was certain of in that moment—the verse Dad had given me so long ago: *I can do all things through Him who strengthens me.*

As I painted Philippians 4:13 along the bottom, I spoke through the tears: "This is for you, Dad. For being the first face I recognized in that lonely hospital bed after the coma all those years ago. For being the first to help me and Dev move to a new house so many times. For being a loving, caring grandfather to my children. For the faith you and Mom taught me at such a young age—a faith that means I don't really have to mourn losing you because we will be together again someday in heaven. I love you, Dad. Everything is going to be okay."

I stared at those words in red for a long time until the studio was engulfed in shadows and it was time to go home.

Early the next morning, I flew back to Beaumont, and every day Mom, Ann, and I sat with Dad in hospice, taking turns reading him Scripture, singing hymns, telling funny stories, and surrounding him with love. Jamey came over from San Antonio, and Ann and I were so glad to have him with us.

On November 12, 2013, shortly after midnight, I lay awake on a cot in the hospice room, listening to Dad breathing nearby. His breathing was slow and labored. With every breath, the space between his inhale and exhale seemed to grow wider. Just as I was about to drift off, Dad inhaled sharply. I leapt out of my cot and rushed over to his side as Dad exhaled his last breath.

I stood beside him in the silence and held his hand. It was an honor to be standing there as Dad passed through that thin space between this life and the next. Dad had been there when I awoke into my new life. It seemed only fitting that I was there when he awoke into his.

Over the next few days, Dev, the kids, and other family members poured in from all over the country. Mom had asked me to speak at the funeral, and I tearfully, yet gladly, accepted. As I thought about what to say, I knew Dad would want me to use this opportunity to tell people about Jesus. He was a man of strong faith, and sharing the gospel message seemed an appropriate way to celebrate his life.

"Whenever Jamey, Ann, or I moved—and we moved a lot," I began, "Dad and Mom always headed right out to help us. Jim Perkins could move you in faster than anyone you could ever imagine—boxes unloaded, pictures hung, bookshelves accessorized—when he left, he wanted to know that his kids were *home* . . . that we were all settled in. And because of my dad's faith in Jesus, we know today that Dad is home. He is with Jesus. He is all settled in."

I then quoted John 3:16 (NIV), "For God so loved the world that he gave his one and only Son, that whoever believes in him shall not perish but have eternal life," and when I looked up, I saw several nods and a few teary faces in the pews.

Before the service was over, Dad's best friend, Ron Wideman, also got up to speak about Dad's faith, the amazing friend he was, and how he would be missed. It was a sentiment all in attendance shared.

Several weeks later, grief still lingered like a heavy blanket I couldn't fling off. Painting was about the only thing I could imagine reviving my spirit, so I returned to the studio, committed to getting back into a routine. After putting on my apron and getting out some brushes, I noticed the canvas I had painted just a few weeks ago leaning against the wall, with Philippians 4:13 painted on it in bright red script. I picked it up, put it on the easel, and studied it for several moments.

During one of my first classes with Andy, he had taught us about the importance of adding an underpainting—a base coat of paint that created a foundation for the layers of paint to come. Artists often use it to create a tonal value for the rest of the painting, to create a map of sorts, or to set a mood.

As I read the verse again, it occurred to me . . . what was Scripture if not the underpainting of my life? The foundation upon which everything else was built? The color that imbued everything else with a deeper, richer hue?

I dipped the brush in a pool of cerulean blue and slowly moved it across the canvas, covering the words. Then I brought in a beautiful orange to add contrast. For hours, I kept working until the red words of Philippians 4:13 were completely faded from view.

But I would always know they were there. And I'd always know why. Whether anyone else saw it there, the Word would always be present.

In that moment, I heard that recognizable voice deep in my heart: *With every one of your paintings, my Word will go out.* It was at once a command and a promise. And I loved it.

From that day on, every piece I did began with a verse from Scripture. I would simply write down whatever verse spoke to me during my quiet time that morning, then I'd take those verses into the studio and start painting.

Before I got started, however, I would write the verse out along one of the stretcher bars on the back of the canvas. It was important to me that people know what the inspiration was behind each piece, even though they couldn't see it through the many layers. Of course, the painting's title always held a clue. For example, *Freely Given* was painted over Galatians 5:22-23 (NLT): "But the Holy Spirit produces this kind of fruit in our lives: love, joy, peace, patience, kindness, goodness, faithfulness, gentleness, and self-control," and *Unstoppable Love* began with John 3:16 (NLT): "For this is how God loved the world: He gave his one and only Son, so that everyone who believes in him will not perish but have eternal life."

It was amazing, just as part of me had died along with my dad, another part had come alive. As grief gave way to revelation, the studio became a place of worship, and every stroke of the brush became an expression of the Word brought to life.

As always, Dad had been right. Everything was going to be okay.

EPILOGUE

I gazed out at the sea of faces, some adorned with knowing smiles, others stunned. I had no idea how much time had passed. "Any questions?"

About half a dozen hands went up. I pointed to a woman standing just to the left of Adrian.

"So . . . did you ever get your memory back?" she asked, eyes wide with amazement.

I caught Dev's eye and winked. "No," I chuckled. "I still have no memory of the years between seventeen and thirty. But that's okay. I came to peace with that ages ago. As I said, there are two ways to look at a blank canvas. You look at it as empty and become paralyzed by what's not there, or you can see it as a starting place to create something new and beautiful." I sought out Callie, Conner, and Casen in the crowd and smiled.

"Yes," I said, pointing to a young man who looked to be about Conner's age, his hair still damp from the rain.

"So then, all of these paintings have a Scripture painted underneath them?" he asked, gesturing around the gallery.

209

"Mm-hmm." I nodded. "This one, for example," I gestured toward the painting directly behind me, "is titled *Lost and Found*. It was inspired by the parable of Jesus and the lost sheep. If you look on the back, you'll see the verse I used as an underpainting written on the stretcher bar, but of course, it's also underneath the painting," I said, running my hand over the many layers. "The verse is Luke 15:5-6:

When he has found it, he will joyfully carry it home on his shoulders. When he arrives, he will call together his friends and neighbors, saying, 'Rejoice with me because I have found my lost sheep.' (NLT)

"The yellow ochre represents the Lord's arms reaching down to earth," I explained, "and the cerulean blue marks represent the sheep. These two blue shapes represent the ninety-nine sheep that the shepherd left to find the lost one. During the season of being lost, we see the blue shapes become hidden in the layers of paint," I continued, gesturing toward the faint shades of blue. "The prominent blue rectangle in the middle of the white paint represents the one lost sheep finally being found. And the red marks are to represent the celebration that occurs when the lost sheep is found."

"How long did that take you?" came a voice from the crowd.

"This one took several weeks. There are quite a few layers involved, and every layer has to dry before the next one can be applied. It's a long process that requires a lot of patience . . . and as some of you know," I said, smiling at Dev, "being patient is hard for me."

Some knowing chuckles emerged from the crowd.

"But over the years that I've been painting, I've learned that every layer is necessary for the next layer to turn out right. And there is inspiration in the waiting."

"I think we have time for one more question," Anne said, pointing at a woman standing directly to the right of Dev. If I wasn't mistaken, she was one of the women he had gallantly ushered in out of the rain.

She looked over at him and bit her lip, stifling a giggle. "So . . . did you fall in love with your husband all over again?" Soft laughter echoed throughout the room.

I glanced at Dev, who smiled widely at me, his eyes crinkling in the corners in that way that had turned my knees to Jell-O since I was seventeen years old.

I took a deep breath and smiled. "I never stopped."

POSTSCRIPT

In the fall of 2018, Dev and I went on a dream vacation to France with five other couples whom we call our "Friends like Family." Life in 2017 had been a veritable whirlwind, with all three of our children getting married within five months of each other and three more solo exhibitions—one at the Umstead Hotel in Cary, North Carolina, one in Chattanooga, and another at Anne's gallery in Charlotte. So by the time fall 2018 rolled around, I was more than ready for a vacation.

The trip was amazing. We indulged in decadent food, marveled at the same French countryside that inspired the paintings of Paul Cézanne, and delighted simply in being together. We saw it all, and every evening as the sun set to rest past the horizon, the twelve of us would gather to reflect on the day's adventure. Jet-lagged belly laughs echoed under the pergola lights in the crisp air of Provence night after night, as did the exchange of God's workings in our lives. And every morning I would awaken overwhelmed with gratitude for God's gift of creation and these amazing friendships. My heart was encouraged, and my mind was at ease. Everything in my life was truly well.

As providence would have it, that trip to France would be the last time I was pain-free.

Shortly after our European adventure, I began noticing an occasional twinge in my hands. Before long, the twinge morphed into a constant ache. By Christmas, I could no longer ignore it, wincing every time I tried to pick up my grandson or open a jar. After wishing away the pain for several months, by February, I had had enough and made an appointment to see my doctor.

That appointment led to another, which led to an MRI. And before I knew it, frightening words, like *rheumatoid arthritis* and *chronic disorder* and *incurable,* were being bandied about. My doctor prescribed a treatment plan in hopes of putting the disease into remission, and I was given a small stack of reading materials before heading home.

As soon as I got out to the car, I brought my hands up to my face—hands that were now being ravaged by a disease I was only just beginning to understand—and wept. I was grieved at the thought of all I might have to give up: an active lifestyle, the joy of picking up my grandchildren without pain, and above all, the ability to *paint*.

So many plans for the following year were already in motion. Multiple galleries were now carrying my paintings, and I still had more to create. All I could think was, *I'm an artist. I need my hands.*

I sat there in the car for a long time, wondering how this latest devastation fit into the plan God had for me. A fury of doubt and chaos whirled in my head. *Why, Lord? Why this? Why now?*

That night at home I curled up in the chair where I do my devotions and where the inspiration for so many of my paintings had revealed themselves to me. Unsure of where to start, I turned to one of my favorite stories—Exodus 14, when Moses and the Israelites are fleeing Pharaoh and his army. Moses calms the Israelites' fears by saying, "Don't be afraid. Just stand still and watch the LORD rescue you today. . . . The LORD himself will fight for you. Just stay calm" (verses 13-14, NLT).

The verses practically leapt off the page. I knew then that I had a choice to make—just like that fateful night in our driveway all those years ago when I was battling alcoholism and the night I was in excruciating pain after my fall, when I looked to God for comfort—I could choose to feed the chaos, or I could turn to Christ for calm.

Just as I had before, I turned to Christ.

A few days later, not wanting to waste any time, I began treatment to kick-start my healing. But the medicine made me feel terrible. Nauseated and weak, my body fought to function, and my hair began to fall out. Worse, not only did the pain persist in my hands, it also spread to my wrists, up to my elbows, and even to my feet.

I'd awaken each day crying out to the Lord, "Please help me!"

But the pain remained, and it was getting harder and harder to stay calm.

Day after day, I headed to my studio to let all my frustrations out on the canvas. Time at the easel usually cured my blues, if only temporarily. But before long, just gripping the paintbrushes was painful. Forced to take frequent breaks, I'd stand still in front of my work, unable to complete the strokes I was visualizing in my head.

If the pain persisted to the point that I couldn't paint anymore, I'd sit down and flip through my art books—most often choosing to escape reality with Cézanne.

While the breaks helped, it was now taking twice as long to finish every painting, and with another solo exhibition coming up in the fall and more than a dozen new works left to do, time was not on my side.

It felt as though painting—the thing I loved more than anything, save my family and God—was literally slipping through my fingers. I felt utterly defeated.

That's when Adrian came up with an idea. One morning she showed up to the studio with a bag full of tennis balls. Each ball had a slit cut down the middle.

"Here," she said. "Put these on the ends of your brushes. It will help you get a better grip." One by one, we began sliding the brushes into the slits Adrian's husband, Michael, had cut in the tennis balls, and I got back to work. The pain was still relentless, but at least I could finally hold on to the brushes long enough to make progress.

Though Adrian's innovative idea was, in many ways, an answer to prayer, my heart continued to harden at the reality of my condition. I might have been able to grip my brushes, but I could not get a grip on the broader situation of how I was going to live with rheumatoid arthritis (RA) or why God would allow painting to be taken away from me again.

Eventually, the questions I demanded answers to led me to reread the Old Testament book of Habakkuk. The prophet did not understand what God was doing either, and like me, he also struggled and cried out to God. Unlike me, however, he eventually found a way to rejoice, and I wanted to know his secret. So I dove in, expectant to read the triumphant ending I must have missed before. But it never came. Habakkuk's situation never changed. His world looked pretty grim, and things didn't seem to be getting better, no matter how much he openly cried out to God:

> Though the fig tree does not bud
> and there are no grapes on the vines,
> though the olive crop fails
> and the fields produce no food,
> though there are no sheep in the pen
> and no cattle in the stalls,
> yet I will rejoice in the LORD,
> I will be joyful in God my Savior.
>
> HABAKKUK 3:17-18, NIV

Then I noticed something. Just like the passage in Exodus, three little words in verse 18 practically leapt off the page: "*yet I will.*"

Habakkuk realized what I had once again forgotten—that true joy could not be found in the contours of his situation, but in God himself. Painting was not the source of my hope and strength, God was. Despite everything that had happened, he was still my foundation.

As I continued to paint that spring and into summer, the phrase "yet I will" rang in my ears—even as the pain in my hands worsened. I sought to find a joy that came from God and God alone, and not from my circumstances improving, my newfound perspective becoming the foundation for my next painting, *And Yet*.

And yet . . . as 2019 drew to a close, the pain persisted. It had been almost a year since the RA symptoms began, and we were no closer to figuring out a course for remission. Even though God continued to speak to me through Scripture, I struggled to be at peace. Every day was a battle, and I was wearing thin, an all-too-familiar feeling.

Then, early one morning, when the sky was still black and the air still cool, God spoke to me through his Word more clearly than he had in a long time. He led me to a passage in Scripture that I had read many times before but that newly captured the physical and spiritual journey he was taking me on. It was Mark 4:35-41, when Jesus calls the disciples out in the boat during a storm.

As I read this familiar passage again, it was as if I was there, standing among the disciples watching everything unfold. I could feel the cool breeze coming off the Sea of Galilee and the disciples' anticipation welling up at the thought of following Jesus to the other side, where miracles were waiting upon the shore. I saw the darkening clouds and felt the first drops of water falling from the sky. My stomach turned as the waves began crashing against the boat and panic began setting in. As the boat filled with water, I could almost feel my feet getting wet, so I scurried with the disciples to the back of the boat to find our Teacher and friend who, despite all the chaos, was sleeping in comfort and total peace. I watched as the other disciples screamed, "Teacher! Don't you care?"—a question I had screamed in frustration many times before, myself.

Just then, Jesus stood and spoke. "Silence! Be still!"

I watched in wonder as the wind stopped, the waves subsided, and the raindrops evaporated in midair. Taking a deep breath, I gazed over the glimmering water now slowly rocking the boat in a rhythm that could have lulled a baby to sleep.

Then Jesus stood in front of me, and meeting my eyes, he proceeded to ask me the same question he asked the disciples: "Marcy, why are you afraid? Do you still have no faith?"

I sat there in my chair and stared down at my Bible, almost tempted to check and see if my feet were actually wet. His pointed question made me feel small and fully known, yet at the same time, full of hope. At that moment I knew he saw me and he cared for me, as he beckoned for me to once again surrender my chaos for his calm, and a familiar refrain echoed in my mind . . .

Everything is going to be okay.

Rheumatoid arthritis is my current storm. I'm still in the midst of it. The pain feels like the waves against the boat—constant and unforgiving, and the howling of the wind echoes the worry in my mind. But now I know that Jesus is in my boat with me, traveling with me as we make our way to the other side, wherever that may be, and however long it takes to get there.

I've held fast to this imagery as we have tried to get my RA into remission. And after many medications, consulting specialists in other cities, and four surgeries to repair damaged joints, I still battle to feel better. Jesus has not cured me of RA. He hasn't taken away the pain. And yet if I could change anything about my circumstances over the past two years, I wouldn't. Because through my pain, I have gotten to know God more richly and deeply than ever before. I would rather be joyful knowing God's faithfulness than be merely happy having my life circumstances work out the way I want them to.

And I am still painting.

I'm grateful God created me to be an artist, because it is through art that I see who God is. Every day when I get to the studio, I start with a blank canvas, but I don't leave it that way. I begin with God's Word, then I add layer upon layer of color, lines, and shapes, allowing some layers to dry completely and some not at all before the next is applied, each layer, stroke, and mark affecting the next, to where, eventually, it is complete. And only I, the artist, know when it's complete. Then I give it a name while signing my own and pray that it brings glory to God wherever it may go.

God is the artist of our lives. We are his blank canvas, and he gives our lives color and texture with every layer applied, each one having its own purpose to the end result. Though not all layers are seen, each of them matter and none are wasted. He uses it all, just as he has used my coma, the memory loss, the alcoholism, the knee injury, and now my RA.

Over the years, as the layers of my life have formed and the joys and sorrows have intertwined, I've learned that God is faithful, that he is relentless in the pursuit of my heart, and that he truly works all things together for good. He is not just God of the universe as I had thought so many years ago. He is also the Lord of my life.

God is the Master Artist. He takes the angles, lines, and splotches of color that look like mistakes and turns them into his perfect, completed work. He knows what he's doing—even if we can't see it yet, and I, for one, can't wait to see the final masterpiece that God will make of my life.

I hope you will trust him to do the same for yours.

AFTERWORD

I vividly remember when the Gregg family first showed up at worship. Dev was warm and engaging, Marcy was bubbly and full of life, and their two boys were clearly loved and cherished. We hit it off, and I hoped they would join the church family I was overseeing at the time.

They did.

Over the next few years, we grew to be friends. The Greggs quickly got involved, serving and reaching out to others. They became a close and important part of our church family.

Then came that terrible day.

I was shocked to learn that Marcy had contracted meningitis. But meningitis doesn't care how young or vibrant a person may be. The meningitis ransacked her body and waged war on her brain. She was immediately placed in ICU, as concern mounted among medical practitioners, family, and friends. No one knew what to do.

I had to leave Charlotte for a speaking engagement, and I didn't have the opportunity to go by and see Marcy before I left. My heart was heavy as I got on the plane to travel. But when I returned to Charlotte, with the wheels of the airplane bouncing off the ground, and the plane screeched to a halt at the gate, something unusual took place. I can count only a few times in my entire life when this has happened. But each time that it did, it was a turning point, a game-changing moment.

I heard the voice of Jesus speaking to my heart—as happens to followers of Jesus. He said in his Word that his sheep can hear his voice (John 10:27). And I knew it was him speaking to me then.

It was the same voice I heard when the Lord called me to ministry: "Don't you know that I chose you from the foundations of the world to proclaim my gospel around the world?" The voice also spoke when I first met my wife, Marilynn: "She is the one you are to marry." (Now, forty-three years later, I know it was true.) Finally, there was the time when God spoke to me during a quiet time, through his Word, that I was going to have a son next year at that time. My heart leapt with joy. And my son David arrived almost a year to the day after I heard that voice.

One sure way of knowing if it's the voice of the Lord is if what Jesus says comes true!

This time, the voice simply said, "Go to the ICU and tell Marcy that the devil cannot have her, and she is not going to die." Admittedly, I shook my head in disbelief. Knocked my temple with my fist a few times. What was going on? Was I going crazy?

But the voice was as clear as a bell. God had spoken to me. And I had to obey.

I entered the concourse and found a pay phone (cell phones were not yet widely available). I called Marilynn to tell her what had happened. "Then you'd better go see Marcy right now," she responded.

I did. I drove straight to the hospital and found my way to the ICU. There were only a few nurses on duty. The lights were dim because it was so late at night. Most of the patients were either asleep or heavily sedated.

I told the head nurse that I was Marcy's friend and pastor and just felt nudged to come pray for her. Though it was past midnight, she didn't hesitate to escort me to Marcy's bed. I sensed she shared my Christian faith. But she also told me, "She is not doing well."

For several minutes, I stared at Marcy. This young woman, emaciated by this terrible disease, lay before me, intermittent beeps from different machines hooked up to her filling the air. Honestly, there was a stench of death as well.

I breathed a deep sigh. I remembered how in John 11 Jesus wept at Lazarus's death, even though he knew the miracle he was about to perform to raise him back to life.

Tears filled my eyes. Jesus hated death, and so did I. It is an evil intrusion into God's once perfect world. It was never his destiny for humankind.

So, I went to war in prayer. I got next to Marcy's ear and said, "Marcy, Jesus wanted me to tell you that the devil cannot kill you. You are to live. Now. Today." I kept praying that prayer over and over again. I spoke Lamentations 3:22-23 (NIV) over her, which says,

Because of the LORD's great love we are not consumed,
    for his compassions never fail.
They are new every morning;
    great is your faithfulness.

Finally, a peace that passes all understanding entered and filled my heart. I knew the battle had been completed. It was finished. Over. I knew Marcy would wake up in the morning.

I got up and went home.

The next morning, I had a meeting at the church with the leaders. Right before the meeting was to begin, Dev called. His excitement could not be contained. Practically yelling, he said that Marcy was awake. She had come out of the coma. The doctors couldn't understand it. They had no medical explanation. Marcy Gregg was going to live.

I rejoiced with Dev and his family. What an incredibly happy moment that was! Then, I whispered a simple "Thank you, Jesus," for I knew that he was the healer and the true hero of the story.

Since then, Marcy has had a long journey to complete recovery. But she has persisted and battled through. She has been challenged by some other trying situations as well. But she has kept fighting. Never giving up. Discovering new paths along the way.

I'm so honored to call Marcy Gregg my friend, and I'm grateful for the years of life God has granted her to share her gifts with the world.

David Chadwick

AUTHOR'S NOTE

Writing a memoir when you suffer from memory loss poses a unique challenge. In sharing my story, I have worked hard to ensure that all of the events are accurate. I have reconstructed scenes and conversations to the best of my ability based on my own and others' memories as well as notes, records, photos, and journals from that time. In a few cases, I have changed or omitted certain names and details out of respect for people's privacy.

There are two ways to look at a blank canvas: you can look at it as empty and become paralyzed by what's not there, or you can see it as a starting place to create something new and beautiful. As I've written in these pages, living with the blank canvas of memory loss has required a great deal of trusting the Lord with all my heart. And yet through it all, I see him painting something beautiful in my life.

ACKNOWLEDGMENTS

Releasing the most intimate parts of my life to the world in written form feels simultaneously terrifying and freeing. My mind swirls, "How did this happen? What will people think?" And yet, my heart knows, "Only you, God. You are the one who orchestrated this process and I must trust you have a plan for it. You are the one who has placed each and every person in my path at the exact right time so that this could come to life." To all the people who have believed in me and this book, who have brought my story to life, I have so much thanks to give.

First, I can confidently say this book would never have happened without Sandi Scott, my assistant and dear friend. Sandi came to me in my studio parking lot years ago after a dream she had. "I feel like I'm supposed to tell you to write a book," she declared. The conversation that unfolded that day became the catalyst to a lot of thought and prayer. People had said this to me before, but this time felt different. A few years later, I let her know I was finally ready and asked her to join me in the journey. Sandi has walked with me every step of the way, and while the book looks different from what we originally thought, she held on with great fortitude until *Blank Canvas* was a reality. Sandi was that "real friend" in Proverbs 18:24 who sticks closer than a brother.

Joy, my literary agent, who gave me a chance when I was just a strange name in her in-box. She believed in me from the first email, and I am so grateful for how she has supported and guided me through this process. Her wisdom has been invaluable, giving me confidence and peace. Thank you for saying yes and bringing all the JOY to the process.

My writer, Katelyn Beaty, who took my words and my life and created a manuscript, giving the book shape and form. Her gift of writing is evident on each page. The first time I ever read through *Blank Canvas*, reliving the moments of my life, I knew Katelyn had done it. She had told it well. Thank you, Katelyn, for taking on this challenge and exceeding beyond my dreams.

Sarah, my associate publisher, another incredible individual who believed in my story before we ever had the chance to meet. She has guided me through the process with such kindness and grace. I am forever grateful to you and your leadership.

Carol, the senior developmental editor, whose creativity, passion, and skill is evident in everything she does. Thank you for pushing for greater and dedicating so much of your time to making sure every detail was just right.

Kara, senior acquisitions editor, who excitedly came to my side in Charlotte to help me through so many important decisions.

Debbie, the developmental editor, whose attention to detail completed the manuscript with thoughtfulness and clarity.

To David Chadwick, you not only prayed, you brought hope into what seemed to be hopeless. I am eternally grateful.

To Dr. Charles Ferree and Dr. Philip DeHoff, as well as all the rest of the diligent medical team that worked to bring me back from the brink of death, thank you.

To Anne Neilson, thank you for believing in my art and giving me my first gallery show. Your support has meant so much to me.

To Adrian, my studio mate and dear friend, thank you for offering to help me so many years ago; you have never stopped showing up for me since. I am forever grateful for how you cheer me on, *Partner*!

To my *friends like family*, words fail to express my gratitude for all the love, grace, and fun we have shared over the years. Through it all, you've been by my side. What a gift each of you are.

To Mom, you loved me fiercely and tenderly and have always been a calming presence in my life. Thank you for always championing my hopes and dreams. I love you.

To my sister, Ann, thank you for the rich laughter and love we have shared. But most of all, thank you for being the ultimate point person in caring for Mom. I could not have written this book without you.

To my children, Casen, Conner, and Callie, you gave my life purpose when I didn't know what the next day would hold. The grace and love you extended when I didn't know the way is a testament to God's mercy in my life. Each of you continues to make me so proud. What a privilege it is to be your mom. Thank you for all your excitement and support through this process.

And it is said the last shall be first . . . Yes! Dev Gregg, you are my best friend and the love of my life. You walked through the story with me the first time, and then stood right beside me as the book was written. Thanks for the hours of reminiscing, the late nights of editing. You were my unwavering pillar of strength. It wouldn't have happened without you, Dev. What a blessing you are to me. Here's to a future full of beautiful memories together!

ABOUT THE AUTHOR

Marcy Gregg is an abstract oil painter whose work is found in private and corporate collections across the United States and abroad. She is also a speaker who shares her story of hope, resilience, and survival. After a coma left her with little chance of recovery, Marcy ultimately regained consciousness but lost much of her memory. Faced with the daunting task of rebuilding her identity, Marcy slowly put the pieces of her life back together, finally returning to her true passion, art. Today, in sharing her story on stages across the nation, Marcy seeks to inspire others by finding beauty in the abstract and hope in the unseen.

Marcy and her husband, Dev, are the parents of three grown children and live in Charlotte, North Carolina.

Visit Marcy online at marcygreggart.com.